CULTURES OF THE WORLD®

LITHUANIA

Sakina Kagda & Zawiah Abdul Latif

Marshall Cavendish
Benchmark

New York

PICTURE CREDITS
Cover photo: © Christophe Boisvieux / CORBIS
age fotostock/Gonzalo Azumendi: 24 • age fotostock/Wojtek Buss: 1, 3, 5, 6, 14, 32, 42, 50, 72, 102, 112 • age fotostock/A. Farnsworth: 37 • age fotostock/Mariano Pozo: 85 • alt.TYPE/ Reuters: 23, 26, 31, 35 • Antanas Sutkus: 4, 9, 11, 13 (top), 20, 22, 33, 38, 52, 53, 57, 59, 60, 71, 78, 82, 90, 94, 96, 98, 100, 103, 104, 108, 110, 111, 115, 117 • Audrius Tomonis: 135 • Bjorn Klingwall: 12, 13 (below), 15, 30, 36, 40, 56, 123, 128 • ELTA: 18, 19, 21, 25, 27, 28, 29, 41, 54, 73, 76, 80, 81, 105, 106, 109, 113, 116, 121, 124 • Hulton Getty: 93 • Hutchison Library: 8, 83, 125 • Kestutis Demereckas: 7 • Lonely Planet Images: 92 • Marka/ Nevio Doz: 122 • National Geographic Images: 43, 67, 101 • Photolibrary/Alamy: 44, 47, 48, 51, 58, 62, 63, 64, 65, 68, 77, 84, 86 • SCR Photo Library: 79, 97, 127 • Stockfood/Bender Uwe: 130 • Stockfood/Bialy Dorota I Bogda: 131 • Topham Picture Point: 66, 88, 95 • Zinas Kazenas: 10, 70, 107, 119

PRECEDING PAGE
The statue of Adam Mickiewicz outside Saint Anne's church in Vilnius.

Publisher (U.S.): Michelle Bisson
Editors: Deborah Grahame, Mabelle Yeo, Crystal Ouyang
Copyreader: Daphne Hougham
Designer: Lock Hong Liang
Cover picture researcher: Connie Gardner
Picture researcher: Thomas Khoo

Marshall Cavendish Benchmark
99 White Plains Road
Tarrytown, NY 10591
Web site: www.marshallcavendish.us

Originated and designed by Times Editions Private Limited
An imprint of Marshall Cavendish International (Asia) Private Limited
A member of Times Publishing Limited

All Internet sites were correct and accurate at the time of printing. All monetary figures in this publication are in U.S. dollars.

Library of Congress Cataloging-in-Publication Data
Kagda, Sakina, 1939–
   Lithuania / Sakina Kagda & Zawiah Abdul Latif. — 2nd ed.
   p. cm. — (Cultures of the world (2nd ed.))
   Summary: "Provides comprehensive information on the geography, history, wildlife, governmental structure, economy, cultural diversity, peoples, religion, and culture of Lithuania"—Provided by publisher.
   Includes bibliographical references and index.
   ISBN 978-0-7614-2087-3
   1. Lithuania—Juvenile literature. I. Latif, Zawiah Abdul. II. Title. III. Series.
DK505.23.K34 2007
947.93—dc22   2007016290

Printed in China

9 8 7 6 5 4 3 2 1

CONTENTS

The old theater square in Klaipeda.

Above: **Art and music come together on a city street.**

Opposite: **Villagers** easily fall into song at a countryside festival.

INTRODUCTION

SITUATED AT THE PRECISE geographical center of Europe, Lithuania once had been among the largest and most powerful countries in Europe. As the power of the grand duchy waned over the centuries, however, it was subjected to invasions and domination by such foreign powers as Germany, Sweden, and Russia. After a brief period as an independent nation between the world wars, Lithuania was illegally annexed by the Soviet Union in 1940.

Lithuania cast off the Soviet shackles in 1991 and since then has looked forward to a new era. It established itself as a democratic nation, restructured and diversified its economy, and joined both the North Atlantic Treaty Organization (NATO) and the European Union (EU) in the spring of 2004. Although many challenges yet remain, both economically and environmentally, Lithuanians forge ahead to integrate themselves into the greater Europe, doing so with an ardent Continental spirit and a strong national pride, firmly maintaining their rich cultural heritage.

GEOGRAPHY

LITHUANIA STANDS AT THE VERY HEART of Europe. The exact geographical center of Europe, certified in 1989 by the French National Geographic Institute, is located 17 miles (27 km) north of the capital, Vilnius. Lithuania's neighbors are Latvia in the north, Belarus in the east and south, and Poland and the Kaliningrad Oblast region of the Russian Federation in the southwest. On the west it borders the Baltic Sea.

Lithuania covers 25,174 square miles (65,200 square km), a little more than West Virginia does. Its surface area is about the size of Denmark or Ireland. It is the largest of the three former Soviet republics bordering the Baltic Sea—Lithuania, Latvia, and Estonia. This trio is often referred to as the Baltic states. They share a similar topography as well as many common cultural elements.

Opposite: **Baltic Sea breakers along the shoreline of Curonian Spit, near Nida.**

Below: **Light snow has just fallen onto the streets of Klaipeda, on the Baltic Sea coast.**

Along the Baltic coast, mile after mile of beautiful white beaches backed by sand dunes and pine forests provide sites for numerous health spas and resorts.

PHYSICAL GEOGRAPHY

The Baltic states are characterized by flat farmlands alternating with low rolling hills formed during the last ice age. Many small rivers, lakes, and scattered pine forests add personality to the landscape. The plains sometimes sink into large tracts of swampland. The region is dotted with ancient city centers ringed with Soviet-era concrete housing projects.

Lithuania can be roughly divided into four ethnographic regions:

- **AUKŠTAITIJA** ("highland" in Lithuanian) in the east is characterized by gently rolling hills, pine forests, and hundreds of lakes.
- **ŽEMAITIJA** is a moderately high area in the northwest and is traditionally noted for its dialect, roadside shrines, and local dress.
- **SUVALKIJA** in the south is to the west of the Nemunas River.
- **DZŪKIJA** is a hilly southern region east of the Nemunas River.

Other main landscape regions include:
- **THE CENTRAL LOWLANDS** is the region in northern Lithuania between Aukštaitija and Žemaitija. This flat land is largely agricultural, although the cities of Šiauliai, Joniškis, and Panevežys are heavily industrialized.
- **THE BALTIC SEACOAST** is marked by sandy beaches and magnificent dunes.
- **THE KAUNAS REGION** is generally flat and agricultural except for the steep hills bordering the Nemunas River valley.
- **THE VILNIUS REGION** is a hilly area with many farms as well as the capital and its surrounding multicultural district. Lithuania's highest point, a 963-foot (294-m) hill called Juozapinë, is located in this area.

Snow piles up along the Baltic shore during Lithuania's long, cold winters.

CLIMATE

The climate in Lithuania is a mixture of maritime and continental. In the coastal zone, the climate is maritime. In the eastern part of the country, it is continental. The mean annual temperature is about 43°F (6°C) with an average temperature in July of 63°F (17°C). There are four distinct seasons. In spring the weather is warm and the land is full of blossoms. Summers have moderate heat, adequate humidity, and a sufficient number of sunny days for vegetation growth. Fall and winter are cold and long.

The mean annual rainfall varies from 21 inches (53 cm) in the central lowlands to 37 inches (94 cm) on the southwestern slopes of the Žemaitija hills. The greatest amount of rain falls in August at the seaside. The growing season is relatively short, varying between 169 and 202 days.

Forests were considered sacred in the ancient Lithuanian religion, and today, Lithuanians retain a deep respect for nature.

RIVERS, LAKES, AND WOODLANDS

Lithuania is a land of notable scenic beauty, with meandering rivers, thousands of lakes, and ancient woodlands rich in wildlife. Forests, including pine, spruce, birch, black alder, aspen, oak, and ash, cover about 32 percent of the total land area. Large tracts of land are bogs and marshland.

Lithuania has a large, dense river network. The waters of the Minija, Musa, Venta, Jura, Sesupe, Dubysa, and Nemunas rivers flow through the country. There are 816 rivers longer than 6 miles (10 km), most of them tributaries of the Nemunas, which flows for 582 miles (937 km). Of this, 295 miles (475 km) is within Lithuania's borders.

Lithuanians like to refer to their country as Nemunasland, due to the great love they have for their river Nemunas. In pre-Christian times, waters and forests were considered to be sacred.

There are about 2,830 lakes with a total area of about 340 square miles (880 square km), making up 1.5 percent of the country's total territory. The largest man-made freshwater lake is the Kaunas Reservoir (Kauno Marios), also called the Curonian Lagoon, a dammed body of water east of Kaunas. The Kaunas Reservoir has an area of 24.5 square miles (63.5 square km). The dam has turned this part of the Nemunas River into a recreational area, and pleasure boats still make the journey from the Kaunas to the Baltic Sea. The deepest lake, Tauragnas, is 200 feet (61 m) deep. Most of the lakes are concentrated in the Aukstaitija hills around Ignalina.

NATIONAL PARKS

The Soviet years contributed to the preservation of nature in Lithuania, ironically, because of Moscow's heavy-handed mismanagement of the country. The percentage of unused land increased after 1940 as the rural population migrated to other countries or was deported to Siberia. As farmlands decreased, forests took over the abandoned land. Thus Lithuania retains large tracts of beaches, woodlands, and wilderness that have vanished elsewhere in Europe because of overdevelopment.

Vast reserves of Lithuania's wilderness are protected by its five national parks. The first, Aukstaitija National Park, was designated in 1974 and covers an area of 100,251 acres (40,572 hectares). Over 70 percent of this park is pine forest. Its beautiful lakes and rivers attract tourists, naturalists, and ethnographers, who study the many ancient buildings and villages in the park.

Dzukija National Park was established to preserve the old villages, the historical and cultural monuments, and the beautiful forests of southeastern Lithuania. Eighty-five percent of the park is covered by woods.

On the Baltic coast is Kursiu Marios (Curonian Lagoon), Lithuania's largest inland body of water. A narrow strip of land called the Kursiu Nerija (Curonian Spit) separates Kursiu Marios from the Baltic Sea. Kursiu Nerija National Park is located on this spit. Until the 15th century the area was covered with forest, but as a result of heavy logging the sand cover was nearly destroyed, and shifting sand dunes sometimes covered whole villages. Attempts to reforest the area to stabilize the dunes have been successful. Today, about 17,297 acres (7,000 ha) of forests protect life on the spit. The other national parks are at Trakai and Žemaitija.

The marshes of Zuvintas Natural Reserve in the Suvalkija region support more than 600 species of plants and 250 birds species. Zuvintas is one of four natural reserves, which are smaller than national parks.

"Where the Sesupe and Nemunas rivers flow, There is our country, lovely Lithuania."

—*Maironis, Lithuanian poet*

A WILDLIFE PARADISE

Because of its large areas of forest and marsh, Lithuania has become the preferred home for a variety of animals and birds. Ducks, waders, terns, and swans can be found in the coastal wetlands, while birds of prey, corncrakes, and white storks inhabit the uplands, and hooded crows haunt the cities. The forests and rivers are home to elk, deer, marten, lynx, boars, beavers, and otters. Occasionally, even brown bears can be spotted in the brush.

Trophy hunting is now becoming popular with sportsmen from other European countries, such as the Germans who visit Lithuania to hunt wolves. Wild game felled by professional hunters has always been popular on Lithuanian menus, but recreational hunting has not been a common pastime in the Baltic states.

Above: **Lithuanians love flowers and will give them to each other for any occasion. Beautiful wild flowers and gardens can be seen all over the country.**

Opposite: **Vilnius is situated in a picturesque valley where the fast-flowing Neris River meets the Vilnia River.**

CITIES

Lithuania's largest cities are Vilnius (population in 2007, 553,000), Kaunas (361,274), Klaipeda (187,442), Siauliai (129,075), and Panevezys (115,604).

VILNIUS Lithuania's capital, Vilnius, is one of the major industrial, scientific, and cultural centers of the Baltic region. The city was founded in 1323 by Grand Duke Gediminas. After dreaming of an iron wolf howling from a hill near the Vilnia River, he invited merchants and craftsmen to settle on the site and build a city. By the 16th century, Vilnius had become one of the major cities of Europe. Vilnius University, founded in 1579, is one of the oldest institutions of higher learning in Europe.

TRAKAI

Trakai was the capital of the grand duchy during the Middle Ages. Today it is a popular resort village in a beautiful region of lakes, forests, and hills west of Vilnius. The heart of Trakai is its castle, probably built by Grand Duke Jaunutis (Gediminas's son) between 1362 and 1382. The complex of defensive fortifications and castle stands on both a peninsula and an island. It is the only island castle still standing in northeastern Europe. The castle is now impressively restored and stands as a monument to the past glory of the medieval Lithuanian state.

The town of Trakai consists mainly of old wooden buildings along with a few modern ones. It is the home of the Karaites, a tribe of Turks brought to Lithuania in the late 14th century by Grand Duke Vytautas to serve as his bodyguards.

The numerous churches that characterize Vilnius were impounded for other uses during the Soviet years, but are now being restored and resanctified. The city's first church, the cathedral, was built in 1387. Rebuilt repeatedly over the centuries, it was the first church to be reconstructed following independence.

KAUNAS Kaunas is Lithuania's second largest city. Its rivalry with Vilnius dates to 1920, when it became the provisional capital after Vilnius was occupied by Poland. Today it is the major commercial center of the country. Kaunas is the most Lithuanian of all Lithuanian cities. Ninety-three percent of its population is ethnic Lithuanian, and much of the old city has survived both World War II and the Soviet period.

HISTORY

LITHUANIA HAS HAD A SHORT HISTORY as an independent nation, but a very long one as a separate culture. Today, as Lithuanians strive to stabilize their young country economically and politically, they look back for inspiration to the time when the Grand Duchy of Lithuania was one of the largest countries in Europe, stretching from the Baltic Sea in the north to the Black Sea in the south, and from Poland in the west nearly to Moscow in the east. More recently, they can recall the tranquil period between the two world wars when Lithuania was an independent and successful nation.

Those periods of greatness have, however, been overshadowed in Lithuania's history by centuries of domination by its powerful neighbors—Poland, Russia, Germany, and Sweden, each of whom has vied for control of this strategically important territory. During these long periods of domination, Lithuanians struggled to maintain their separate identity and culture. They have preserved their language, their religion, and their traditions in spite of repeated intrusive attempts to obliterate all traces of ancient Lithuania.

Above: **Gediminas Tower, the oldest relic of the settlement of Vilnius, was built by Grand Duke Gediminas in the 14th century.**

Opposite: **The gothic Trakai Castle, on an island in Lake Galve, was built in the 14th century.**

THE EARLY LITHUANIANS

The prehistoric inhabitants of the Baltic region were nomadic hunters and, at a later time, farmers. Around 2500 B.C. Indo-European tribes spread across the region that is now western Russia, Ukraine, Belarus, and Poland, eventually concentrating along the Baltic shoreline. They merged with the indigenous population and formed a number of distinct tribes in the territory that is now Lithuania. At the end of the first century A.D., the Roman historian Tacitus described the people living around the Baltic Sea in his history of Germany. He noted that they traded in amber and that they were able farmers, saying that in the growing of corn and other crops they worked "with more patience than is customary among the lazy Germans."

From the second to the fifth century, the Baltic tribes enjoyed a golden age in which they developed a trading empire that webbed northeastern Europe. During the ninth and 10th centuries, Vikings from Scandinavia

In its heyday in the 15th century, the Grand Duchy of Lithuania was the most powerful state in central Europe.

launched raids on the prosperous coastal regions of the Baltic, and the Baltic tribes and the Vikings alternately fought and traded with each other.

The 10th century also saw the start of feudalism in the Baltic region and the emergence of the Lithuanians—the largest tribe—as dominant on Lithuanian territory. Naturally barricaded by impenetrable forests and thousands of lakes, Lithuania remained largely isolated until the 14th century.

THE GRAND DUCHY

During the 13th century, German crusaders invaded the Baltic region in a bid to conquer and Christianize the last remaining pagan tribes in Europe. The Knights of the Sword and their successors, the Teutonic Knights, overpowered the tribes of Latvia and Estonia, creating the country of Livonia.

As the other Baltic tribes fell to the German knights, only the Lithuanians succeeded in maintaining their independence. In 1236 Mindaugas unified the small feudal states of Lithuania into a duchy. The united Lithuania struck a powerful blow against the Knights of the Sword at Siauliai. In 1251 Mindaugas adopted the Catholic faith in order to be crowned king by Pope Innocent, hoping that as a Christian he would not be a

THE HOUSE OF LIUTAURUS

Most of the grand dukes of Lithuania have belonged to a single dynasty. Their reigns were: Vytenis (1295–1316), Gediminas (1316–41), Jaunutis (1341–45), Algirdas and Kestutis (1345–77), Jogaila (1377–92), Vytautas the Great (1392–1430), Svitrigaila (1430–32), Sigismund (1432–40), Casimir (1440–92), and Alexander (1492–1506).

target of the Knights. In the face of continual problems with the crusaders, however, he later renounced Christianity. Mindaugas was assassinated in 1263.

The formation of the state was completed by the grand dukes Traidenis (who reigned 1270–82) and Vytenis (1295–1316). Vytenis left a large state with clearly defined policies to his brother Gediminas (1316–41). Under Gediminas, the Lithuanian territory was expanded as far as Kiev and the Black Sea.

ALLIANCE WITH POLAND

The Lithuanian leaders were successful in resisting the ongoing attacks by the Teutonic Knights, but under increased pressure in the late 14th century, they decided to ally themselves with Poland, which was also fighting the crusaders. In 1385 Lithuanian nobles arranged the marriage of Grand Duke Jogaila of Lithuania to Princess Jadwiga of Poland. The match was quite advantageous—Jadwiga's husband would become king of Poland—but there were strings attached: Jogaila must become a Christian and convert his whole empire as well. Jogaila agreed, was baptized as Ladislaus, and assumed the crowns of Poland and Lithuania. Lithuania was the last European country to adopt Christianity.

Grand Duke Jogaila became king of Poland when he married Princess Jadwiga in 1385.

After the marriage of Jogaila and Jadwiga, Polish feudal lords tried to abolish the Grand Duchy of Lithuania, but their efforts were resisted by the Lithuanian aristocracy, and Lithuania maintained its separate identity. Jogaila's reign in Poland (1386–1434) started the long period of a Lithuanian-Polish common history, which survived until the 18th century.

VYTAUTAS THE GREAT

After Jogaila, the position of grand duke of Lithuania was given to his cousin Vytautas, who became the last of the great Lithuanian rulers. He drove back the Turks, and under his rule, which flourished from the late 14th to the early 15th centuries, the grand duchy became one of the largest states in Europe.

The Teutonic Knights continued their attempts to conquer Lithuania. Finally, in 1410, the Lithuanians and the Poles defeated them at the Battle of Tannenberg, ending the Knights' ambitions in the Baltic.

Poland put its cultural stamp on Lithuania. The Lithuanian nobility were quick to appreciate that they would gain personally from Poland's rigid and efficient social and political order. The pre-Christian religion vanished as Roman Catholicism took hold. The nobility spoke Latin at court and Polish elsewhere.

Weakened by increasing fights with Russia, in 1569 Lithuania joined with Poland to form the Union of Lublin, "a commonwealth of two nations." Lithuania retained its territory, legislation, treasury, and army, but shared Poland's king and government. The merger did not help strengthen Lithuania, though, and the grand duchy slowly declined.

The Grand Duchy of Lithuania reached its greatest expanse during the reign of Vytautas the Great.

RUSSIAN OCCUPATION

The disintegration of the grand duchy in the 18th century led to an economic, social, and political crisis exacerbated by wars with Sweden,

THE VYTIS

The state emblem of the Republic of Lithuania is the Vytis (VEE-tis), the White Knight. It shows a white knight in armor on a white horse, holding a raised sword in his right hand. A blue shield on the left shoulder of the knight has a gold double cross.

The charging knight was first used as the state emblem in 1366 on the seal of Grand Duke Algirdas. With minor stylistic changes, the Vytis remained the state emblem of the Grand Duchy of Lithuania until the 18th century. When Lithuania was annexed by the Russian Empire in 1795, the Vytis was incorporated into the imperial state emblem.

In time, the charging knight came to stand for a patriotic knight chasing an intruder out of his country. Banned under Soviet rule, the Vytis became an enduring symbol of the Lithuanian drive for independence.

Baltic tribes of the ninth–12th centuries:
Lithuanians
Curonians
Semigallians
Selonians
Samogitians
Nadruvians
Prussians
Jotvings
Skalvians
Latgalians

Russia, and Turkey. Lithuania was partitioned three times (in 1772, 1793, 1795), with different countries claiming parts of it. In 1795 Lithuania was absorbed by the Russian Empire, except for a small part that was incorporated into Prussia.

In reaction to peasant uprisings, Russia began an intensive process of Russification. The goal was to eradicate all traces of ancient Lithuania. Landholding rights were limited to followers of the Russian Orthodox religion. Vilnius University was shut down in 1832, and only Russians were admitted to schools above the elementary level. Starting in 1864, the Lithuanian language and the Latin alphabet in which it was written were banned.

Although Lithuanians tried to resist the Russian occupation, their uprisings in 1831 and 1863 failed. In their wake, Russification became more intense, but resistance continued. For example, Lithuanian-language books were printed in the Prussian portion of Lithuania and secretly smuggled into Lithuania, where they were quietly circulated. From 1891 to 1893, 37,718 Lithuanian books and newspapers were confiscated by the Russian border police. From 1900 to 1902, the number was

56,182. In 1883 the first Lithuanian newspaper, *Ausra*, was published. When that was brutally crushed, *Varpas* sprang up. The ban on the press was finally lifted in 1904.

PROCLAMATION OF AN INDEPENDENT STATE

Popular demands for Lithuanian autonomy continued to surface. When World War I turned Lithuania into a battlefield, in the fall of 1915, its entire territory was occupied by Germans, who had already defeated the Russians. Resistance continued to mount, though, and on February 16, 1918, Lithuania proclaimed its independence. Germany recognized the new state in 1918 as did Russia in 1920.

Nonetheless, Lithuania continued to face problems with its neighbors. In October 1920 Poland occupied Vilnius, causing the capital to be transferred to Kaunas. In 1921 the duchy was admitted to the League of Nations. A democratic constitution was adopted in 1922, and the litas became the currency.

Nationalist Party leader Antanas Smetona became Lithuania's first president. He served as president from 1919 to 1920, and then again became president in late 1926 after seizing power in a military coup. One year later, in 1927, he dismissed parliament and became the authoritarian leader of Lithuania until 1940.

Antanas Smetona, the first president of independent Lithuania. Though an authoritarian leader, he presided over a prosperous period.

During these 22 years of independence before the Soviets overran the country, Lithuania's economy grew to compete with those of Western European countries. Lithuanians later looked back on that time with nostalgia, and they longed to return to it all through the 50 hard years that followed as a Soviet republic.

SOVIET AND GERMAN OCCUPATIONS

Flowers and candles are placed along railway tracks in memory of the 350,000 Lithuanians who were deported to Soviet labor camps.

On June 14, 1940, the Soviet Union issued an ultimatum to Lithuania, demanding the resignation of its government. It had to yield, and on the night of July 11, 1940, more than 2,000 people were deported, including members of the government who were deported, too, or executed, and a new pro-Soviet government was installed. Within a few days, Lithuania was incorporated into the Soviet Union. The incorporation was not recognized as legal by any Western government. In June of 1941, another 34,000 Lithuanians were deported to Siberia.

The Russian occupation was overcome by the German army, which occupied Lithuania from 1941 until 1944. During that time, the Nazis executed about 175,000 Lithuanian Jews and 16,000 ethnic Lithuanians, and deported another 36,000 Lithuanians to labor and concentration camps in Germany. The large Jewish community in Vilnius was almost entirely wiped out.

In 1944 the Soviet Union once again took Lithuania under the umbrella of its Communist regime. There were mass deportations, in which the Soviets sent more than 350,000 Lithuanians to labor camps in Siberia. Many of those deported died along the way. Farms were reorganized into a collective farm program, and the Lithuanian economy became subordinated to the demands of the greater Soviet economy. Religion was suppressed, as were other aspects of Lithuanian culture. Many ordinary freedoms were eliminated.

By the late 1980s the Soviet economy was in a desperate condition. The Soviet leader, Mikhail Gorbachev, introduced the reform policies of glasnost (openness) and perestroika (restructuring). Under these new policies, Soviet citizens were encouraged to voice their opinions and to participate in the reform of the Soviet system. This new openness led to the clamorous emergence of independence movements in many of the Soviet republics. One of these was Lithuania.

REESTABLISHMENT OF INDEPENDENCE

On February 7, 1990, the Lithuanian Communist Party proclaimed the 1944 Soviet annexation to have been illegal. They were supported by Sajudis, a proindependence party. In national elections held in 1990, Sajudis won a majority in the parliament. By the Act of March 11, 1990, the Lithuanian parliament declared the restoration of the independence of the Republic of Lithuania. Vytautas Landsbergis, the new leader of parliament, formed a cabinet of ministers under Prime Minister Kazimiera Prunskiene, and adopted a constitution. The Soviet government announced an economic embargo and sent tanks to Vilnius, but faced with vociferous international disapproval, they agreed to negotiate.

Former Lithuanian president Algirdas Brazauskas casting his voting ballot at a polling station in Vilnius, October 8, 2000.

Little progress was made in the negotiations, and on January 13, 1991, Soviet tank units seized radio and television stations. Fourteen Lithuanians were killed in the confrontation. In August of 1991 an attempted coup of the Soviet government failed in Moscow, and Lithuania's independence was recognized internationally soon afterward. Lithuania was admitted to the United Nations in September 1991 and joined the Council of Europe the following year. In June the litas was reintroduced as the national currency. In 2004 Lithuania joined the North Atlantic Treaty Organization (NATO) and the European Union (EU).

GOVERNMENT

LITHUANIA IS AN INDEPENDENT democratic republic. The foundations of the political and social system are stipulated in the constitution of the Republic of Lithuania, which was adopted in October 1992. The constitution declares that state power in Lithuania is "exercised by the Seimas [parliament], the President, the Government, and the Judiciary."

THE CONSTITUTION

On May 18, 1989, the Lithuanian Supreme Soviet—the highest legislative body in Soviet Lithuania—adopted a declaration of Lithuanian sovereignty that asserted the supremacy of Lithuania's laws over those from Moscow. A general election in February and March 1990 resulted in a pro-independence majority in the Supreme Soviet, and that body affirmed the restoration of Lithuanian independence. The Lithuanian Supreme Soviet was renamed the Supreme Council. It brought back the pre-1940 name of the country (the Republic of Lithuania) and adopted the Provisional Fundamental Law of the Republic of Lithuania, which restored portions of the Lithuanian constitution of 1938. It established the rights, freedoms, and duties of the country's citizens.

Above: **A political rally organized by a Lithuanian workers' union.**

Opposite: **Tourists outside the President's Palace in Vilnius, the capital city.**

A senior voter casts his ballot at a polling station in the village of Seduva, southern Lithuania, in a democratic election in December 1997.

A new constitution was approved in a national referendum in October 1992. It created a strong presidential system with a legislature of 141 elected representatives and a Council of Ministers headed by a prime minister.

THE SEIMAS

The highest state authority is the Seimas (SAY-mahs), formerly called the Supreme Council. About half of the members of this legislative body are elected in individual constituencies and the other half are elected by nationwide vote according to proportional representation. With the approval of the Seimas, the president of Lithuania will appoint the Council of Ministers, which is the highest authority of executive power. The Council of Ministers is headed by the prime minister. Supreme judicial authority is vested in the procurator general, who is also appointed by the president with the approval of the Seimas.

The Seimas, the highest expression of state power in Lithuania, in session.

As the highest state authority, the Seimas has the power to adopt laws, consider proposals of programs produced by the government, approve the budget of the government, establish the state institutions provided by the law and appoint or dismiss their directors, and settle other issues pertaining to state power.

In the elections of October 1992, 141 deputies were elected to the Seimas. Deputies' terms of office are four years. They must be at least 25 years old with a permanent residence in Lithuania.

The chairman of the Seimas or his deputy presides over Seimas meetings. In 1992 Ceslovas Jursenas was elected chairman. In 2007 the post was held by Viktoras Muntianas. The Seimas structure and procedure are determined by the Seimas Statute, which is the act establishing the Seimas. The Seimas headquarters is in Vilnius.

ALGIRDAS BRAZAUSKAS

The Sajudis (Lithuanian Reform) movement won a majority in parliament in 1990, but a year later, as winter set in, many Lithuanians still had no heat or hot water in their homes. The voters were unhappy about unemployment, high prices, and fuel shortages, and when elections were held in October and November 1992, the proindependence Lithuanian Democratic Labor Party (LDLP), formerly the Communist Party, was returned to power.

Algirdas Mykolas Brazauskas (pictured right) was elected president of Lithuania in the first direct presidential elections, in February 1993, and served until February 1998. He decided not to run for a second term and retired from politics. Subsequently he also resigned as a member of the LDLP. In July 2001, however, Brazauskas made a comeback when he was appointed prime minister, a post he held until June 2006. Brazauskas served as chairman of the Lithuanian Social Democratic Party until May of 2007. The Lithuanian Social Democratic Coalition was made up of the LDLP and the Lithuanian Social Democratic Party (LSDP). Brazauskas's coalition party won 20 seats in the 2004 Seimas election.

In April 2004 then president Rolandas Paksas was impeached on the grounds that he maintained links with the Russian mafia.

THE PRESIDENT

The president of the Republic of Lithuania is the highest official of the state. The president in 2007 was Valdas Adamkus, who had held the post since July 2004. He represents the country and is elected by citizens of Lithuania for a term of five years on the basis of universal suffrage by secret ballot. The president upholds the constitution and the laws and also performs other duties:

- resolves major issues of foreign policy and conducts foreign policy jointly with the government
- signs international treaties, submitting them to the Seimas for ratification
- with Seimas's approval, appoints the prime minister and empowers him or her to form the government (Council of Ministers), and confirms its composition
- appoints and dismisses state officials

- submits candidates for the supreme court and the constitutional court for the evaluation of the Seimas
- with Seimas's approval, appoints and removes the chiefs of the armed forces and security service
- confers the highest military titles
- proclaims a state of emergency as provided by law
- makes annual reports to the Seimas on the "state of the nation" in Lithuania, including its domestic and foreign policy
- announces elections
- signs and announces laws passed by the Seimas, or sends them back to the Seimas for reconsideration
- issues acts and decrees
- exercises such other powers as provided by the constitution

Lithuanian soldiers in a dress parade. The country did not have an army during the Soviet era.

Vytautas Landsbergis was leader of the Sajudis movement when it gained a majority in parliament in March 1990. He became the first leader of Lithuania after independence.

THE GOVERNMENT

The government of Lithuania is composed of the prime minister and 13 ministers. The prime minister is appointed or dismissed by the president with the approval of the Seimas. Ministers are also appointed and dismissed by the president upon the recommendation of the prime minister.

The government controls affairs of the country, ensures state and civilian security, and carries out laws, resolutions of the Seimas on the enforcement of laws, and decrees of the president. It also enters into and maintains diplomatic relations with foreign countries and international organizations and performs the duties specified in the constitution and laws.

Since coming to power, the government has shouldered a twofold challenge. It has had to establish the legal, institutional, and regulatory framework of an independent democratic state. At the same time, it needed to restructure the centralized economy into a free-market economy while reducing economic dependence on the former Soviet Union.

THE JUDICIAL SYSTEM

The judicial system consists of a constitutional court, a supreme court, a court of appeals, and district and local courts. The constitutional court consists of nine judges appointed for nonrenewable terms of nine years. It determines whether laws enacted by the Seimas, or actions of the president or Council of Ministers, are in conformity with the constitution.

The Seimas appoints three judges for the constitutional court and another three for the supreme court. Three judges for the court of appeals are appointed by the president with approval of the Seimas. Judges of district and local courts are appointed by the president. Public prosecutors conduct criminal cases on behalf of the state.

CORRUPTION AND CRIME

The Lithuanian government is not without its troubles. Politics still bears a strong resemblance to that of the Soviet era, and many Lithuanians are becoming disillusioned with the current system. Only 45 percent of eligible voters participated in local elections in 1996. In 2004 a similarly low turnout was seen when only 43 percent of Lithuanians cast their votes. Few legal constraints govern politicians' business interests, and there is widespread public concern over political corruption. In 1995 two of Lithuania's largest banks went bankrupt and their chairmen were charged with fraud. The prime minister at the time, Adolfas Slezevicius, was implicated in the financial scandal and was stripped of his office within months.

The judiciary and the police staffs were trained during the Soviet era. Corruption is increasingly widespread, resulting in a wave of organized crime, burglary, and car theft. Street crime is also on the rise.

A citizen appraising an election appeal of Valdas Adamkus, one of the main candidates for Lithuania's presidency in 1997.

ECONOMY

SINCE INDEPENDENCE in September 1991, Lithuania has made steady progress in developing a market economy. To ensure economic stability after the breakup of the Soviet Union, Lithuania and the other two Baltic states, Latvia and Estonia, launched a program of land reform and market-oriented economic reforms in November 1991. The economic changes encompass price structure, government spending, foreign trade, banking and monetary policy, competition, taxes, ownership, and privatization laws. Today over 80 percent of state property has been privatized, and trade is diversifying, with a gradual drifting away from the former Soviet Union to international markets, mostly within the European Union (EU).

During the Soviet occupation, 5 percent of exports were sent to the West; in 2005 exports to the EU were nearer to 65 percent. A main reason for the shift in export focus to the West was the collapse of the Russian ruble in 1998. Lithuania's economy fell into negative growth, and budget deficits amassed. As the economy recovered from the crisis, Lithuania looked West for its trading partners. Lithuania facilitated easier trade with the EU by pegging the litas, its national currency, to the euro at LTL 3.4528 for EUR 1 in February 2002, in anticipation of eventually adopting the euro.

Lithuania's economic profile shows a strong inclination toward the services sector, which includes transportation, shipping, and wholesale and retail trade. Principal exports and imports are mineral products,

Above: **The ice-free seaport Klaipeda is the center of the fishing industry.**

Opposite: **Most rural farmers in Lithuania do not use modern farming machinery, and it is still common to see horses, carts, scythes, and pitchforks—agrarian time capsules from other days.**

Lithuania's most important natural resources are peat, arable land, gravel, construction sand, quartz sand, dolomite, clay, limestone, brick clay, and some relatively small deposits of oil that are found mostly offshore under the Baltic Sea.

machinery and equipment, chemicals, and light industrial products such as textiles and food products. The country's current main trade partners are Russia, Germany, Poland, Latvia, Estonia, the Netherlands, Sweden, the United States, the United Kingdom, France, and Denmark.

Lithuania has a skilled workforce with expertise in modern technology developed during the years when the Baltic states were exploited as an economic and industrial laboratory by the Soviet Union. Its total workforce stood at 1.61 million in 2006, with a majority employed in the services sector (60 percent). The country is superbly positioned for international trade as it has access to major adjoining markets. To its east lies Russia, Lithuania's main import and export partner, and to its west is all of central Europe, one of the world's most prosperous regions.

LIFE AFTER THE SOVIET UNION

The breakup of the Soviet Union in 1991 severely disrupted the economy of Lithuania. The Soviet Union had previously supplied Lithuania with heavily subsidized supplies of raw materials as well as guaranteed markets for the goods manufactured in Lithuania.

Lithuania, however, has received considerable international support for its economic reform. It gained membership into the International Monetary Fund (IMF) and World Bank in April 1992. The European Bank for Reconstruction and Development, the World Bank, and the IMF guaranteed loans in 1993 to bolster the recovering nation's economy.

In June 1995 Lithuania signed the Europe Agreement with the European Union to prepare for becoming a member of the EU. By May 2004 Lithuania had achieved this goal. Prior to that, the European Union had already provided considerable encouragement as well as financial

THE SEARCH FOR ENERGY

Lithuania has yet to reach its potential in developing such renewable energy sources as hydropower (water), solar, wind, and geothermal power. Currently only 9 percent of its total primary energy is from renewable sources. Lithuania is heavily dependent on the Ignalina nuclear power plant to supply its industries with the necessary power. The plant was run on two powerful reactors, providing 87 percent of Lithuania's total energy needs. The plant is old, however, and similar in construction to the Chernobyl plant in Ukraine that exploded in 1986. This is why the

EU was insistent that Lithuania shut down the plant as one of the conditions to its entry into the EU. The first reactor was shut down in 2005, with the second one expected to close by 2009. The governments of Estonia, Latvia, Lithuania, and Poland agreed in 2006 to together construct a new nuclear power plant at Ignalina by the year 2015.

Lithuania thus must search for other sources of energy, as the country is severely lacking in fuel resources. Although peat deposits supply some of the country's energy needs, other fuel materials like oil, natural gas, and coal are imported. Until July 2006, an oil refinery in Mazeikiai obtained crude oil from Russia and exported the refined products from the seaport of Klaipeda—the Mazeikiai refinery did not supply energy for the country itself. But Russia has since cut off its oil supplies, citing environmental risks of a leak and repairs on the pipeline as the reason. In December of 2006 the nation's sole refinery was sold to the Polish company PKN Orlen.

Lithuania's other sources of power include the Kaunas Hydroelectric Power Plant and the Lithuanian Power Plant (LPP). LPP, the Kaunas Combined Heat and Power plant, and Lithuania's transmission grid are all undergoing modernization to increase their power-generating and -delivery capacity.

support. Assistance was concentrated in the four key areas of agriculture, such as finance, labor (human resource development), infrastructure development, and regional development programs. In May 2001 Lithuania had gained membership in the World Trade Organization, becoming its 141st member.

AGRICULTURE AND FISHING

Lithuania has always been agriculturally self-sufficient. In recent times, though, there has been a drop in agricultural production as Lithuania focused its attention more toward a service-based economy. Agriculture yields less than 10 percent of the country's exports today. Of a total land area of 16 million acres (6.5 million ha), only 4.32 million acres (1.75 million ha) are used for food and feed crops.

The most important sector of the farming industry is livestock. Cattle, sheep, pigs, and chickens provide meat, eggs, and dairy products for export as well as domestic consumption.

Wheat, barley, and oats are grown in the western and central part of the country. Potatoes and sugar beets are also valuable products. Flax is an important product of the eastern part of the country. The stalks of this plant are used to make linen cloth, and flaxseeds are used as a dietary supplement and to produce linseed oil.

The fishing industry is also profitable. Herring, cod, and flounder are caught in the Baltic Sea, the Barents Sea, and the Atlantic Ocean. Carp and eel come from Lithuania's many bountiful inland lakes and ponds.

INDUSTRIES

The main branches of Lithuania's industry are oil processing, machinery and transportation equipment manufacturing, electronics, textiles, chemicals, plastics, forest products, and food processing. Food processing is primarily based on local meat and dairy supplies. Other industries include the production and packing of sugar, bread, confectionery, alcoholic products, tobacco, and vegetable oil.

Vilnius and Kaunas are industrial

A Danish company out-sources all its sewing to a factory in Kaunas, Lithuania, because of the lower costs in man-power.

centers, with textile mills producing knitwear, carpets, stockings, leather goods, footwear, and linen, cotton, and silk fabrics. Substantial amounts of these products are exported to other European countries. Siauliai, the fourth-largest Lithuanian city, is an industrial center for the production of foodstuffs and beverages, precision lathes, television parts and components, computers, and bicycles. Raw materials are imported from Russia, and 9.4 percent of its finished products are exported to the Commonwealth of Independent States, which includes Russia and most of the former

Soviet republics. Some 90 percent of Siauliai's exports, however, are to other European countries.

Lithuania produces television and audio equipment, refrigerators, vacuum cleaners, electric engines, drills, and some agricultural machinery. The construction materials industry is based on local raw materials and satisfies local needs in cement, brick, glass, roofing supplies, thermal insulation, and nonmetal substances. Cement and bricks are also exported. The chemical industry, dependent entirely on imported raw materials, specializes in fertilizers, plastics, household chemicals, and rubber products. Local timber is processed for both local consumption and export markets—as of 2007, forest products make up about 5 percent of the country's exports.

THE AMBER COAST

Lithuania was once known as the Amber Coast because of its great deposits of amber, a translucent fossilized tree resin valued for its subtle beauty. Amber can be found scattered like pebbles along the beaches of the Baltic shores. For centuries it has been a source of wealth for the Balts, who traded it as far away as Egypt. Tutankhamen's tomb included jewelry made with amber. A peculiarity of the resin is that before hardening, the ooze attracts insects, which may become trapped inside. One can sometimes look closely at a piece of amber and see inside a perfectly preserved mosquito or gnat from ages past.

PRIVATIZATION

In the 1950s and 1960s, the Soviets forced the collectivization of agriculture and industry. One of the major changes brought about by independence was the privatization of these state-owned enterprises and cooperatives.

Lithuania's successful privatization program was achieved by the use of vouchers, which were issued to all citizens in 1991 on the basis of age. The vouchers were exchanged for ownership shares in former state assets. Such investment decisions were often handled by professional managers. Today, Lithuania's private sector accounts for more than 70 percent of the economy's output.

Some of the agricultural cooperatives were split into small farms, returning the farms mostly to village families who had prior claims to the land. In 1997 family farms made up 75.8 percent of the country's agricultural production, although these farms average only 18 acres (7.3 ha) in size. Agricultural companies, on the other hand, manage less than 5 percent of agricultural land. By June 2005 Lithuania had about 129,000 agricultural holdings. Of these, 22 percent were made up of less than 12.36 acres (5 ha) of agricultural land, while 5 percent used 123.55 acres (50 ha) or more.

TRANSPORTATION

Transportation in Lithuania is good and continually improving. The Via Baltica, the highway that links Lithuania to Latvia and Estonia in the north and to Poland in the south, runs through Lithuania via Kaunas. Major airline flights arrive daily at Vilnius International Airport. Lithuania has 95 airports, of which 33 have paved runways. In 2004 aviation carried

Lithuanian Airlines provides a comprehensive service to the East and West.

about 591,000 passengers, and passenger traffic at airports was 1.1 million.

In the same period, the railways carried some 6.98 million people and 45.6 million tons of freight. Railway lines total 1,242 miles (1,998 km), crisscrossing the country. The Jonava railway station, a short distance from Kaunas's Karmelava International Airport, links to the Kaliningrad Region, Latvia, and the Klaipeda Seaport for convenient passenger and cargo transportation.

The port of Klaipeda is ice-free and operates year-round. It transships a considerable variety of goods, such as machinery, oil, coal, cement, grain, sugar, fish, and other foods. In 2005 the port handled almost 22 million tons of cargo, mainly from trade with Belarus and Ukraine. Klaipeda has 19 stevedoring (docking) companies, ship-repair and shipbuilding yards, a bulk terminal, a commercial harbor, and a lucrative fishing port.

Such integrated transport systems, a key geographical position, and the historical relationship with the former Soviet republics are making Lithuania of considerable interest to Western companies. IBM, DHL, Xerox, Olivetti, and Minolta have come to Lithuania. Other key foreign investors include Scandinavian TeliaSonera (telecommunications), Paroc (construction materials), Storaenso (wood products), DSV (sea transport), American Kraft Foods and Mars (food processing), and Philip Morris (tobacco products). German car giant Volkswagen-Audi and French carmakers Renault and Peugeot have opened showrooms, the Swiss Vast Group has opened a chain of stores across the country, and Scandinavian companies are initiating joint ventures.

WORKING LIFE

Workers at one of the shipyards in Klaipeda.

In 2005 the working-age population of Lithuania was 1.6 million, of which 1.47 million were in active employment. In the same year, 132,900 Lithuanians were registered as unemployed. Women accounted for fewer than half of all unemployed workers.

The main sectors of employment in Lithuania are manufacturing and industry (around 21.1 percent of the labor force); agriculture, hunting, and forestry (16.9 percent); and services, which includes transportation, storage, and communications (62 percent). Government and state-owned enterprises employ some 38.6 percent of the workers.

Since independence, Lithuanians have a 40-hour workweek. There is a national minimum annual leave of 28 days. Extended annual leave of 35 days is granted to the disabled and to people under 18 years. Employees working under great physical or mental strain, those in high-risk professions, and certain others are given 58 days annual leave. Child-care leave is available for parents with children under 3 years old.

ENVIRONMENT

THE LITHUANIAN LANDSCAPE, like those of most countries of the former Soviet Union, suffers from much neglect and abuse. Political apathy and general technological backwardness throughout the Soviet years have resulted in damaging environmental problems that continue to the present day.

Since its independence, nevertheless, and even before its entry into the European Union, Lithuania has been conscientiously tackling its pressing environmental issues. Some of the measures undertaken include establishing a realistic system of waste management, the cleanup of contaminated military sites, and the establishment of parks and nature reserves. Lithuania is working hard to ensure the continued preservation and sustainability of its environment.

Some of the country's environmental management bodies include the Ministry of Environmental Protection, established in 1994; the Department of Land Management and Biological Diversity; and the Joint Research Center. Another organization that helps in the support and realization of environmental projects is the Lithuanian Environmental Investment Fund. All environmental entities in Lithuania comply with the Environmental Strategy of the Republic of Lithuania, taking into account the norms and standards of the European Union.

Above: **A stork guarding its nest in rural Lithuania.**

Opposite: **Graceful trees growing around Druskonis Lake in Druskininkai.**

A dammed section along the Nemunas River, the well-loved waterway for all Lithuanians.

WATER AND SANITATION

WATER Lithuania is possibly the only country in Europe using groundwater resources as its only source of potable water. Yet nearly a perturbing third of the country's water, including rivers and lakes, is polluted. Uncontrolled dumping by industries and the lack of sewage treatment facilities are the main causes of water pollution. Experts estimate that Lithuania's largest inland body of water, the Curonian Lagoon, is about 85 percent contaminated with effluents from industrial and domestic waste.

This is because of the high population density around the Baltic coast, and the industrial center of Klaipeda is just north of the lagoon. As the Curonian Lagoon lies just inside the eastern shoreline of the Baltic Sea, runoff currents from the sea are common, bringing in with them additional pollution from neighboring Russia and Poland. Industrial waste from Belarus also pollutes rivers that flow into the Curonian Lagoon. In 1998 about 800,000 Lithuanians were identified as drinking water from wells where traces of nitrates were present.

Water and sanitation

Currently, about 70 percent of Lithuanians have access to potable water from the public water supply system, but small towns and rural settlements are still supplied with water of poorer quality as they are usually not connected to the public water supply and sanitation networks. With assistance from the EU, as well as funds from the Lithuanian budget, more than 1 billion litas have been allocated to wastewater treatment projects. This aid made possible the renewing of older treatment plants and the building of some new ones.

The completion of the wastewater treatment plant in Klaipeda has helped to reduce the concentration of pollutants in the lagoon. In all, five sources of pollution have been eliminated, and pollution was prevented in a 148-acre (60-ha) area. Between 1998 and 2005 Lithuania also managed to halve the concentration of pollutants in the Baltic Sea near its coast.

SANITATION There are about 800 municipal landfills in Lithuania, but they are neither environmentally friendly nor properly operated. Flammable hazardous wastes, including solvents and materials polluted with oil, are incinerated in boilers ill equipped to do the job. At present, there are 22 sites—storing such hazardous chemical wastes as discarded dried-up varnish and paint—still pending investigation and proper disposal of their contents. A number of small sites also are largely neglected because of an inadequate system of waste management. Every year 1.4 million tons of solid domestic waste are dumped, as the collection of glass, paper, and cardboard waste for recycling is poorly organized.

A proper system of waste management has only recently been established. New domestic dump sites are being set up in Kedainiai and Kaisiadorys, and major Lithuanian cities have begun to use separate containers for glass, plastics, metals, and kitchen waste. With financial

The biggest wastewater treatment plant is in Vilnius. It treats an average of 4.05 million cubic feet (114,800 cubic m) of wastewater a day, or 1,480 million cubic feet (41.9 million cubic m) yearly.

backing from the EU, Lithuania will be able to install modern waste management infrastructure in most of its major cities. Furthermore, all 800 municipal landfills will be closed by 2012, and a new burning facility will be built for hazardous waste management.

SOVIET LEGACY

Lithuania's contaminated soil is another major contributing factor to the country's polluted groundwater woes. Aggressive industrial production through the use of chemical fertilizer and pesticides during the Soviet years has seriously contaminated Lithuania's soil with biogenic and toxic chemicals. Scant attention was paid to soil pollution in the pursuit of agricultural gains.

In the 1990s Lithuania had about 4,500 tons of obsolete pesticides stored in 800 storage depots. Since independence, the government has been proactive in collecting information on agricultural soil contamination and collaborating with organizations to manage the use of chemicals on its soil. Over 3,000 tons of pesticide had been transported to Germany by 2007 for safe disposal. By then, only 21 out of the 96 remaining depots were still environmentally unsafe.

Former Soviet military activities and their use of oil products and heavy metals have also left 167,444 acres (67,762 ha) of Lithuanian land contaminated. The cleanup of these military sites, leading to the reutilization of the land, is a costly, ongoing project, even with funds from the EU. The state budget for the management of still contaminated sites is also limited. Although the restoration of every military site in Lithuania is not required by law, the government does require the cleanup of 10 specific military sites that are perceived to pose a public threat. The estimated cost for that project is expected to be $733 million.

AIR POLLUTION

One of the relatively new environmental concerns that Lithuania faces today is air pollution from cars and trucks. Although the quality of air in recent times has marginally improved, at one point about a third of Lithuanian territory was suffused with polluted air at any given time. About 362,000 tons of pollutants from vehicles are released into the atmosphere each year. In Vilnius, traffic congestion has become acute, especially during the morning and evening rush hours.

The other main sources of air pollution are industrial centers and cities such as Vilnius, Kaunas, Klaipeda, and Jonava, where fertilizer and cement factories as well as power plants are concentrated. Lithuania's total carbon dioxide emission in 2001 was 11.8 tons (12 metric tons). The cement industry alone produces 294,278 tons (299,000 metric tons) of airborne pollutants per year. The Siauliai region is the most heavily polluted in Lithuania, contributing 40 percent of the general emissions for the entire country because of the presence of a thermal power plant.

Air pollution has not only damaged about 68.4 percent of the nation's forests but has also added to the problem of acid rain. Forests affected by acid rain are found in the vicinity of Jonava, Mazeikiai, and Elektrenai, Lithuania's main chemical, oil, and power-generating sites.

In June 2005 the government approved a strategy for the development of the Lithuanian transportation system. Some of the aims include tightening the requirements for exhaust gases and noise levels; prohibiting car traffic in old towns, central parts of cities, and centers of high-density

In the city, increasing number of vehicles on the road contribute to air pollution, although nonpolluting electric trams do help the problem.

A pristine forest in the Cepkeliai Reserve in southern Lithuania.

parking; encouraging the use of clean fuel; and promoting the use of electric vehicles and hybrid vehicles for city travel. The government has also set up the Sustainable Development Strategy for its industrial sector. Today there is a reduction in industrial carbon dioxide emissions through the implementation of ISO 14001, an environmental management standard that allows for the increased efficiency of industrial processes, while reducing gasses emitted as by-products and improving health and safety conditions.

Lithuania has signed treaties to reduce its greenhouse gas emissions and to gradually reduce and prevent air pollution. It also has ratified treaties on climate change and ozone layer protection.

LITHUANIA'S FORESTS

Forests are of great economic, ecological, cultural, and social importance to the people of Lithuania. Forests cover 32 percent, or about 4.9 million acres (2 million ha), of the entire country. The state manages 49.3 percent of these forests, 32.8 percent are held in private hands, and 17.9 percent or 914,290 acres (370,000 ha) are state forestland reserved for privatization.

Lithuania's Law on Forests was approved in 2001. The law calls for forest management that includes equal regeneration, protection, and

NATURE RESERVES

There are four small marshland areas in Lithuania—Cepkeliai, Kamanos, Viesvile, and Zuvintas—that have been declared nature reserves. About 35 wild animal, 200 bird, 11 to 20 fish and 600 to 800 flora species are under their watchful eye. A special permit is required to even enter these reserves.

The Cepkeliai Reserve in southern Lithuania has the country's largest and oldest marshland. A wide variety of berries, birds, insects, and reptiles find haven at this reserve. It covers 20,947 acres (8,477 ha), of which 14,053 acres (5,687 ha) are marshlands. It was established in 1975.

The Kamanos Reserve in northern Lithuania was established in 1979. Under protection are its bogs, 556 species of higher plants, and 123 species of mosses. Twenty-six of those plants are noted as rare or endangered species. Wildlife is also diverse, with 36 species of mammals, 120 species of birds, 3 species of reptiles, 6 species of amphibians, and two species of fish. Access to this park is carefully monitored, and any type of commercial activity is strictly prohibited.

Established in 1991, the Viesvile Reserve in the Karsuva lowland includes 7,947 acres (3,216 ha) of great natural beauty. It is ringed with an additional 6,076 acres (2,459 ha) of protective buffer zone. The reserve has a uniquely homogeneous ecosystem as it was hardly touched by Lithuania's economic activity in the Soviet interval.

The fourth protected area, the Zuvintas Reserve is composed of 30,678 acres (12,415 ha) of woodlands, marshes, and water. It was established in 1937 to preserve the flora and fauna of Zuvintas Lake as well as its bogs and swamps. Some 250 species of birds such as the heron and mute swan can be found there, and the reserve is also the habitat of 580 species of higher plants. About 20 beaver families make their homes at this reserve.

use regardless of ownership. One of the conditions of the law states that clear-cut forest areas must be reforested within three years after cutting.

Many of Lithuania's original animal and plant species are now extinct because of past indifference. Acid rain due to air pollution from industries and power plants from neighboring countries is also a contributing factor. Currently, five mammalian species and four species of birds are threatened, including the European bison, marsh snail, and Russian desman (a mammal similar to a muskrat). Nevertheless, Lithuania is determined to preserve its forests' riches. Some of Lithuania's recent triumphs include a substantial increase of woodlands, an enlargement of protected areas, and the preservation of biological diversity. Lithuania also adheres to the Ramsar Convention, protecting wetlands, biodiversity, and the conservation of endangered species.

Independent from its 5 national parks and 4 nature reserves, there are 30 regional parks dotted all over Lithuania.

LITHUANIANS

INDO-EUROPEAN SETTLERS ARRIVED in the Baltic region around 2500 B.C. They organized into several tribes, and in the course of time these tribes merged, generating today's ethnic Lithuanians. The tribes were the Lithuanians, the Jotvings in the Suvalkija region, the Semigallians and the Selonians in the north, the Curonians in the far west, and the Samogitians (or Zemaitians), who inhabited the Zemaitija region. Today these tribes and their descendants—the people of Lithuania and Latvia—are referred to as Balts. This term was derived from the name of the Baltic Sea and was first applied during the 19th century.

Above: **Eating ice cream with happy young friends in the city of Vilnius.**

Opposite: **A smiling Lithuanian girl wearing flowers in her hair might be greeting visitors to her country.**

From the 13th century, Lithuania was settled by other nationalities as well, including Poles, Germans, Russians, and Tatars (Mongols). At the beginning of the 14th century many Jews settled in Lithuania, where they found asylum from religious persecution in other European countries. In the second half of the 18th century, Russian Orthodox Christians also seeking sanctuary from such persecution settled in Lithuanian villages.

The character of today's Lithuanians has been influenced by decades of intense Soviet repression. Many talented and educated Lithuanians fled the country in 1944, and many more died under harsh German and Soviet occupations. In spite of a concerted attempt to stamp out Lithuanian culture and identity, the Lithuanians have cherished their traditions and still point proudly to the historical greatness of their country. They feel themselves to be the natural leaders of the Baltic region, although they may also feel some apprehension about what the future holds for their struggling new country.

The population of Lithuania is estimated at 3.6 million. The largest population group is the ethnic Lithuanians (83.45 percent). Next are the Poles (6.74 percent). Most of the Poles reside in Vilnius and southeastern Lithuania. Russians, who live mainly in urban areas such as Visaginas, Vilnius, and Klaipeda, form the third-largest ethnic group (6.31 percent). People of other ethnic groups are few: Belorussians (1.23 percent) and others like Latvians, Jews, Tatars, Gypsies, and Germans all told make up another 2.27 percent.

POLES

The Polish presence in Lithuania dates back to the Middle Ages, when Grand Duke Jogaila's marriage to the Polish princess Jadwiga joined the two countries. Many upper-class Lithuanians adopted the Polish language and Polish customs, and the distinction between the two groups became blurred. Until World War II, ethnic Lithuanians were a small minority in Vilnius, fewer than the Poles and the Jews. Many important Polish cultural figures came from Vilnius, such as writers Czeslaw Milosz and Adam Mickiewicz, and Jozef Pilsudski, the ruler of Poland between the world wars.

As a result of the historical conflict between the two countries over Vilnius, many Lithuanians used to fear that the Poles wanted to reclaim Vilnius. In turn, their anxiety about Lithuanian nationalism impelled many Poles to support the Soviets during the independence struggle, another factor that further aggravated relations. International treaties signed in the 1990s have ended this prolonged conflict and eased relations.

Above: **Ethnic Russian singers enjoy performing at Lithuanian music festivals.**

Opposite: **Polish Lithuanians in traditional dress gather on many special occasions.**

RUSSIANS

Lithuanian Russians mostly migrated to Lithuania after World War II, a time when Lithuania underwent rapid industrialization. There are some 220,000 Russians nationwide today. About 50 percent of the population in the Visaginas municipality is ethnic Russian—about 15,000 people. Most of them belong to the Russian Orthodox Church. Because of the painful Soviet occupation, some resentment toward Russians lingers among ethnic Lithuanians. The problem is not as acute as it is in the other Baltic states, however, where the percentage of Russians is much higher.

Approximately a million Lithuanians live outside their homeland, of whom more than 76,000 live in Russia, 33,000 in Latvia, 25,000 in Poland and 11,000 in Ukraine. There are about 120,000 Lithuanians in Ireland today. Many Lithuanians reside in Marquette Park, a neighborhood of Chicago. The 2000 U.S. census counted 11,000 people of Lithuanian direct ancestry in Chicago, although nearly 80,000 in the metropolitan area claimed some Lithuanian ancestry. Lemont, a suburb of Chicago, also has a large Lithuanian-American community.

THE JERUSALEM OF THE NORTH

Jews began settling in Lithuania in the 14th century, when they were invited in by Grand Duke Vytautus. By the 18th century, Lithuania was considered to be one of the most important centers of Jewish culture in the world. Vilnius was known as the Jerusalem of the North because of its large Jewish presence—30 percent of the population of the worldly capital—with a large number of synagogues and Hebrew schools. At the time, Jews made up 7.6 percent of the Lithuanian population. Later in the 18th century, Vilnius was a center of Jewish Orthodox resistance to the Hasidic movement then sweeping Eastern Europe, and before World War II, Vilnius was the hub of Yiddish publishing.

The Jewish community was almost entirely obliterated by the Nazis during the German occupation of Lithuania. More than 130,000 Vilnius Jews died, and the rich Jewish culture that had flourished in Vilnius since the Middle Ages was wiped out. The Nazis interned and exterminated

Jews at Fort Nine, a Nazi concentration camp in Lithuania, only a few miles outside Kaunas. In addition, Jews from all over Europe were herded there to await execution. The prison cells still exist, and there is now a museum and a monument to the victims on the site.

In 1989 there were just some 12,400 Jews in the entire country. Many of those Jews who were not killed in the Holocaust had joined the steady flow of emigrants away from the Baltic states. Apart from economic reasons, the urge to emigrate was also provoked by memories of Lithuanian participation in the Holocaust—the first massacres in Lithuania were conducted entirely by Lithuanians without direct German involvement—and by perceptions of contemporary anti-Semitism. Today only about 4,000 Jews remain in Lithuania. Their communities are concentrated mainly in Vilnius, with smaller ones in Kaunas, Klaipeda, and Siauliai. A Jewish studies program has recently been established at Vilnius University.

TATARS

Some 50,000–100,000 Tatars, also known as Mongols, came to Lithuania during the time of Vytautas the Great (1350–1430), who was their protector. The Tatars were renowned for their valor in battle—their main occupation became fighting the enemies of Lithuania. In return, Lithuanian rulers gave them protection and religious freedom. Later, the Tatars took up agriculture, animal husbandry, and the processing of animal skins. A famous Lithuanian Tatar was General Maciej Sulkiewicz, who headed the Cabinet of Ministers of the Republic of Crimea in 1918. In 1997 the 600th anniversary of the settlement of Tatars in the Grand Duchy of Lithuania was celebrated. A year later, a spiritual center was reestablished for the ethnic Tatars' Sunni Muslims.

Ethnic festivals in Vilnius attract striking displays of traditional dress.

TRADITIONAL DRESS

The Lithuanian national costume dates only from the early 19th century, although it differs considerably from one region to another in ornamentation and color. From the early 20th century, the national dress, particularly for women, has been influenced by urban tastes. Today it is usually worn by participants in folk music and dance concerts and in religious processions and ethnic festivals and processions. Most garments are produced commercially according to designs drawn by professionals, but the tradition of making one's own is again becoming popular.

Men's traditional clothing consists of a shirt, trousers, vest, lightweight coat or jacket, overcoat or sheepskin coat, hat, and footwear. Shirts are full-sleeved and made of thick linen, with a cotton stand-up collar embroidered in black and red. Before the 20th century, trousers were made of homespun linen, wool, or cotton. Winter trousers are dark-colored, and summer ones are white or white on blue. They are tied with a sash around the waist. Strips of cord or leather are appliquéd to the edging, cuffs, collars, and pockets of coats and jackets, which are worn over vests. Many kinds of caps are worn by men in rural areas, but in warm weather straw hats are preferred.

There are several kinds of traditional footwear in the countryside, but the most striking shoes are perhaps the solid wooden *klumpes* (KLOOM-pus), worn by men and women.

In the past, the clothing of a Lithuanian woman reflected her industry, accomplishment, and taste. Traditional woman's dress consists of a skirt, blouse, bodice (a tight sleeveless garment worn over the blouse), apron, and sash. Outer garments are a sheepskin coat and a scarf. Unmarried women generally wear ribbons and beads in their hair instead of scarves.

Women of the Aukstaitija region prefer light colors, particularly white. Their skirts are mostly checked, and the aprons have horizontal red patterns at the bottom. The background of an apron is usually checked, striped, or patterned in cat-paw motifs. The fronts of blouses, sleeves, collars, and cuffs are embellished with red stripes.

The Zemaitian women's attire includes several articles of sharply contrasting colors—a tailored bodice, a vertically striped skirt, and an apron. Shawls are worn over the head and shoulders. *Klumpes* are the typical Zemaitian footwear.

Women's traditional clothes in the Klaipeda region are dark in color, and the blouses have a gathered neckline. The bottom portion of sleeves, the cuffs, and a wide band below the shoulders have colorful designs such as clovers, tulips, or oak leaves. Their sashes and stoles have intricate patterns. The stole is made of two panels with a narrow lengthwise insertion embroidered with white plant motifs. Almost all women carry a decorative handbag called a *delmonas* (dayl-MOH-nus), which is fastened at the front or side of the waistband.

Amber necklaces, the beautiful fossil resin found in Lithuania since ancient times, are an important accessory for every woman wearing traditional dress.

57

LIFESTYLE

LITHUANIANS HAVE RETAINED many features of their traditional lifestyle in spite of the Communist occupation, which muzzled national traditions. Due to modernization, emigration to foreign lands, urbanization, and higher levels of education, some events have been simplified and are practiced only as rituals. Although their original meanings may have been forgotten over generations, more and more Lithuanians are trying to bring the old ways of living back into their everyday lives.

RURAL LIVING

Rural living has always been an important part of the Lithuanian way of life. Today, many of the old Soviet collectives have been broken up into small farms, much as the land was apportioned during the prosperous

Left: **Country women taking a break for lunch in the fields.**

Opposite: **Lithuanians relaxing at a café in Gedimino Pospektas, the main street of Vilnius.**

Most people in rural areas live in modern, prefabricated houses that all look very much alike. Recently, however, farmhouses have become more varied as owners build them according to individual preferences and from original designs.

period in the early 20th century, and rural Lithuanians, numbering about 1.2 million, are returning to a more traditional lifestyle.

Some city dwellers are also turning toward self-sufficiency on the land. During the Soviet era, small plots of land measuring 6,460 square feet (600 square m)—about 80 feet by 80 feet—were provided for company and factory workers. Densely planted with fruit trees, vegetables, herbs, and flowers, they still sprawl around the towns and cities. Some people built simple weekend cabins on their allotments. Since independence, planning regulations have been loosely enforced, and even solid brick houses are appearing on these plots.

In addition to a house, actual farms have barns for cows, pigs, poultry, and fodder, as well as granaries, a well, a sauna, a kitchen garden, and an orchard.

LITHUANIAN INTERIOR

The interiors and furniture of Lithuanian houses are well designed for the needs of domestic life. The colors and textures of different woods are used to good advantage, giving homes a warm, cozy look. Sunlight filtering onto walls and ceilings shows off the woods' natural textures.

Lithuanians use moderate amounts of bright colors in their furniture, curtains, paintings, flooring, and linens. The furniture includes chests for fabrics and clothes, tables, benches, chairs, beds, cupboards for food and utensils, and wardrobes for clothing. Wooden furniture is decorated with paintings, printed ornaments, or relief carvings.

Altars, religious icons, and statues also adorn the interiors of homes. Paintings on wooden panels or canvas, depicting saints and scenes from the Bible, are hung on walls.

Farms are encircled with maple and linden trees. Oaks, considered to be the most beautiful trees, are planted at the front, birch trees near the barns, and rowan trees, a type of ash, along the fringes of the property. Almost every house has a cross erected by the roadside. A flower garden is a traditional feature of every Lithuanian house and farm.

During the long, dark winters, fish are caught in the frozen lakes, and licensed professionals hunt wild game. The arrival of the stork signifies the return of spring. When the snow melts, the swamps rise and the rivers burst their banks. Some houses on the delta of the Nemunas River are built on stilts to escape the floodwaters.

Urban dwellers like to visit the countryside in summer. Some city children spend the whole summer with relatives in the country. Weekend visitors go home with baskets and bags filled with wild berries and other fresh goods.

The late summer harvest is hard work. Agricultural machinery is limited and out of date, and horses and carts are still seen in most of Lithuania. Scythes and pitchforks are used as much as they ever were. The unpredictable weather affects the harvest, so nobody is sure what will appear in the shops. This, coupled with the uncertain agricultural economy, means that city people view their neat little patches of land as insurance against hunger and deprivation.

Lithuanians love birds. A birdhouse, or a cartwheel fixed to a tree or rooftop for a stork to build a nest in, is a ubiquitous part of the rural scene. Houses where birds make nests are considered safe resting places for travelers because the birds indicate that a good person lives there. Swallows nesting under the eaves are believed to protect the house against lightning.

The modern Europa Tower shopping complex in Vilnius.

URBAN LIFE

Some 2.3 million Lithuanians live in cities and towns. Around 80 percent dwell in the five largest cities—Vilnius, Kaunas, Klaipeda, Siauliai, and Panevezys.

After World War II the urban population grew steadily as the cities were rebuilt and new industries sprang up. Today, housing is a mix of single-family houses and apartment buildings.

The Soviet regime built the huge housing projects that now surround almost every town in the Baltic region. These mass-produced and badly assembled concrete towers are very different from the attractive, historic city centers that tourists visit. Faced with a chronic lack of housing, families still live in cramped accommodations, sometimes with members of their extended family or even sharing a kitchen and bathroom with other families in communal apartments. As of 2001, there were only 356 housing units per 1,000 people, with an average living space of about 70.54 square feet (6.55 square m) per person. In the United States average space per person is about 645.83 square feet (60 square m). In June 2005 the government adopted a resolution to modernize some of these apartments. About 70 percent of the apartments will be considered for rehabilitation, and city governments are also looking into constructing new housing projects.

Street crime is increasing in the cities, and car theft is common. Still, conditions are better than those in many parts of the former Soviet Union. Public transportation in the cities is well developed, with some 60 bus lines and 19 trolley car lines in Vilnius, transporting some

500,000 passengers every workday. Lithuania has the most advanced telephone system in the former Soviet Union, and unlike some cities in neighboring countries, it is safe to drink the tap water.

THE ROLE OF WOMEN

Lithuania was the first country in Europe to define the rights of women not simply as mothers or potential mothers. This was the result of a matrilineal tradition in the ancient tribes and a society in which men were absent during long periods of war. The Statute of Lithuania of 1529 established the principle of individual legal responsibility and equality for women in the eyes of the law, irrespective of religion or marital status.

Families celebrating a harvest festival on the streets of Vilnius.

In present-day Lithuania, women work in all occupations. Wage discrimination on the grounds of sex, age, race, nationality, or political convictions is illegal. Still, women's participation in political life and public administration is low. The number of women in parliament since independence has never been more than 20 percent. Currently, there are only 31 women in the 141-seat parliament and 2 women ministers.

Nevertheless, Lithuanian women have excelled in politics, literature, and archaeology. Marija Gimbutas achieved fame as an archaeologist, ethnologist, linguist, and author of numerous books. Among her published books are *Ancient Symbolism in Lithuanian Folk Art, The Language of the Goddess, The Civilization of the Goddess,* and *The World of Old Europe.*

THE FAMILY

Prior to World War II, many extended families, composed of grandparents, parents, children, uncles, aunts, and their children, lived and worked together as units in villages. Often servants and other nonrelatives lived in the house and were treated as part of the family. Extended families are still found, both in cities and the countryside, as a result of the prolonged housing shortage.

Today, however, most Lithuanian families are nuclear families, consisting of a married couple and their children. The father is usually the head of the household. Given the rise of single-parent families today, though, many single mothers are now the head of the household.

Traditionally, a woman went to live with her husband's family when she married, and daughters-in-law were readily welcomed as members of the family.

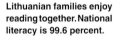

Lithuanian families enjoy reading together. National literacy is 99.6 percent.

BIRTH

It is still thought that evil spirits and improper behavior can harm an unborn baby or the expectant mother. For these reasons, pregnant women have to observe a number of restrictions. At the same time, family, friends, and neighbors—in fact the whole village— protect and indulge the whims and fancies of expectant mothers.

Childbirth is shrouded in secrecy, and people talk of pregnancy and the actual birth by using such euphemisms as "The oven fell apart at Petra's" or "It is a joyous day at Antana's."

A baby girl on a park outing with her older siblings.

The birth of a child is considered a blessing. Soon after the birth, the women among the new parents' relatives and neighbors visit the mother and child. Each visitor brings a symbolic gift. No visitor comes empty-handed, as that is considered to jeopardize the child's good fortune. In many areas, it is customary to bring an omelet or a buckwheat loaf.

A child's christening is held two or more weeks after the birth. Godmothers and godfathers play important roles in the event. The selection of these godparents is considered crucial because it is thought that the child absorbs their temperaments and habits. This process binds families together, as the godparents take on part of the responsibility of raising the child.

A Lithuanian mother takes some of her daughter's first loaf of bread to the local sauna to treat her neighbors and to boast of her new helper, who has come of age.

Ice cream—one of the small pleasures of childhood—is sold in parks and street cafés everywhere.

CHILDHOOD RITUALS

It is through ritual introduction to adult responsibilities that the young are considered to have come of age.

The baking of her first loaf of bread marks the onset of puberty and is the symbol of a girl's coming of age. On a Friday evening, the mother gives some rye flour to her daughter. The daughter mixes the dough and leaves it to ferment overnight. On Saturday morning, the girl kneads the dough, then allows it to rise. She lights the oven, forms the loaves, incises a cross on the top of the first, and puts the loaves in the oven. When they are done, she removes them. The bread is eaten that day by her family with great ceremony.

In rural areas, fathers teach their sons how to harness and unharness horses, yoke and unyoke oxen, and to plow their first furrow alone.

GOING TO SCHOOL

A new national education system was introduced in Lithuania in 1990. Education is compulsory from age 6 until 16, and it is free of charge at all levels. General schools go from 6 to 14 years, and secondary schools from 15 to 17 years. Lithuanian is the main language of instruction, although there are schools at which classes are taught in English, Russian, Polish, or Yiddish, with some schools offering classes in two or more languages. There are 27 institutions of higher education in Lithuania, including the venerable Vilnius University, Vytautas Magnus University in Kaunas, Vilnius Technical University, and the Lithuanian Academy of Sciences.

Adult literacy is very high—99.6 percent: 99.7 percent for men and 99.6 percent for women. In 2002, 27 percent of government spending went toward education.

A couple on their wedding day celebrating with family and friends.

WEDDINGS

Modern Lithuanian weddings are full of humor and good-natured teasing. Although they have been simplified, they retain the main elements of traditional weddings.

After a civil ceremony and a solemn wedding in the church, the wedding party heads for the bride's home for a feast. The way is barred, however, by the bride's family and friends with ropes of flowers. The last of the garlands is stretched across her parents' gate. The groom's friends buy their passage with candy and a bottle of whiskey. They also distribute candy to children along the way.

The bride's parents meet the newlyweds at their threshold with bread, salt, and wine glasses filled with water—all symbolic of a fulfilled life.

Inside, the seats for the bride and groom are adorned with more flowers and garlands, but they cannot sit down as the chairs are already occupied by neighbors dressed as gypsies, a matchmaker, a bride (a man in disguise), or a bridegroom (a woman in disguise). Both groups start haggling over the price of the seats, and after much banter and laughter the seats are sold for a bottle of whiskey.

One dish is deliberately made bitter, and on the first bite the guests start singing a traditional song: "Bitter, bitter is the food. It will be sweet when the bridegroom kisses the bride." The guests then volunteer lots of instructions to the bridegroom on how to do it well.

A very important wedding role is played by the matron of honor, who is usually a married woman closely related to the bride. She remains next

EXECUTING THE MATCHMAKER

Arranging marriages with the help of the matchmaker was once widely practiced in Lithuania, but today the young choose their own life partners and matchmakers rarely play a part in their social lives and courtship. Nowadays, matchmakers are only characters acted out at weddings to bring fun to the occasion.

A wedding tradition that has survived is the mock execution of the matchmaker. The bride's friends and siblings decide that the matchmaker had exaggerated the description of the groom's looks and possessions, so they decide to execute the matchmaker. The sentence varies—he may be condemned to be burned by water, or frozen to death on the stove, or to be sent away to a hayloft with all the girls of the neighborhood. He accepts his sentence and asks to be allowed to say good-bye to all the ladies. He then smears his face with soot and tries to kiss every woman and girl in the house. The wittier the matchmaker, the funnier is his "execution." In the end, the bride's mother takes pity on the poor man, and as a sign of her forgiveness throws a towel across his shoulders. The matchmaker is thus saved, and the guests hang a dummy instead.

to the bride and groom, making sure all the customs are followed, and acts as a symbolic guardian to the bridal pair to ensure that no evil might damage their health and fertility.

At the end of the reception, the bride says good-bye to her parents, family, garden, neighbors, and friends, and asks for forgiveness if she has ever hurt them by word or deed. This is a rather sorrowful part of the celebration, accompanied by the bride's family's *raudos* (RAO-dohs), or farewell songs.

Parents prepare dowry chests for their daughters well in advance. These chests are made from the wood of a tree in which storks nest, so as to bring luck and fertility. The chests are filled with jewelry, documents, letters, money, a rue wreath, medicinal herbs, clothes for the firstborn child, linens, bedclothes, rolls of fabric, woven sashes, and other handmade articles. The size and beauty of her dowry chest is an indication of the bride's wealth, status, taste, and industry.

This elderly man must have seen many changes in Lithuania during his lifetime transforming the country dramatically.

HEALTH

Until 1940, health care was provided by both state and private facilities. The Soviets introduced comprehensive state-funded health care. After Lithuania's independence in 1991, a National Health Concept was adopted that shed the Soviet system and called for extensive reforms. The 1992 constitution guarantees the right of all citizens to receive old-age pensions, disability pensions, and assistance in the event of unemployment, sickness, or widowhood. Since 1997, a compulsory national health-care insurance plan covers all residents.

There are about 3.97 doctors and 7.62 nurses for every 1,000 people in Lithuania, as compared with about 2.8 doctors and 3.3 nurses for every 1,000 people in the United States. Doctors are well trained, but they are forced to work with limited supplies of medical instruments, materials, and medicines.

THE ELDERLY

Great respect is given to elders in Lithuanian society. A younger person would respectfully address an elderly person as grandmother, grandfather, uncle, or aunty, never by his or her name.

In modern Lithuania, where both parents work, grandparents often take care of their grandchildren. In fact, they may move in with their children and grandchildren. This gives the grandmother and grandfather an opportunity to teach the third generation about Lithuanian customs, beliefs, traditions, folktales, crafts, games, dances, and music, and to retell stories of their ancient heritage and mythology. Nursing homes are rare in Lithuania.

FUNERALS

In villages, the dead lie in state at home for three days. In towns and cities, they lie in the funeral parlor for two days. The footpath in front of the house or funeral parlor is strewn with pieces of spruce branches.

The dead person is dressed in his or her best clothes and laid in a coffin, which is placed in a room with beautiful woven bedspreads fixed on the walls. A cross, some pictures of saints, and two burning candles are placed at the head. Wreaths and ribbons inscribed with words of condolence are also hung on the walls or placed on the sides of the coffin.

Family and friends keep vigil throughout the days and nights. Silence is observed as much as possible, as it is thought that though the spirit separates from the body at death, it does not leave the house until the deceased is carried away. In the evenings the neighbors gather to pray and sing hymns written by local poets. After the prayers, a funerary meal is served. If the family owns a pig, it is butchered for this meal.

Wooden grave markers in a Lithuanian cemetery.

In southeastern Lithuania, the tradition of *raudos* at funerals still survives. Laments, spoken or sung by professionals or relatives, express the sorrow of the living and the sad plight of the children left behind, as well as recalling the good deeds of the deceased.

In the country, the dead are usually buried in the morning. Before closing the lid, a cross is burned onto the lid with a hallowed candle. It is traditional to give the dead person a last kiss. After the coffin is lowered into the grave, everyone there throws in a handful of earth. Throwing flowers into the grave is a new gesture. After burial, a cross is pressed onto the top of the mound and wreaths and flowers are laid on it.

71

RELIGION

THE LITHUANIANS WERE THE LAST Europeans to relinquish their ancient beliefs and rites. The country converted to Christianity only in the 14th century. Today the main religion of Lithuania is Roman Catholicism. While most ethnic Lithuanians and virtually all Poles are Roman Catholics, there are also small pockets of Lutherans, Calvinists, and some other Protestant denominations. Adherents of Russian Orthodoxy and the Old Believers (Old Ritualists) are mostly Russians. There are some Tatars, who are Muslim, and a small Jewish community.

Opposite: **The ornate altar of Saint Casimir Church in Vilnius.**

Below: **Roman Catholic children at a solemn church service.**

PRE-CHRISTIAN RELIGION

There are still a few Lithuanians who practice the ancient religion, and many others who combine some of the old traditions with Christianity. This group is observing the Day of Gediminas around the time of the autumn equinox.

The religion of the ancient Lithuanians was based on animism—the belief that all things have a spirit. Ancient Lithuanians worshipped objects and natural phenomena. Cults devoted to forests and fires were widespread. There were sacred fields and forests that no one was allowed to enter or work in. Certain kinds of trees, such as oaks and pines, held special powers. As late as the 18th century, Catholic officials were still chopping

THE LITHUANIAN GODS

The ancient Lithuanian religion was polytheistic, meaning that many gods were worshipped. The pantheon of Lithuanian gods is rich and diverse. The god of bright daylight, Dievas, the supreme deity, was a kind, gentle, and wise god. The most popular god was Perkunas, the god of thunder. He was master of the atmosphere and the "waters" of the sky, as well as fertility, human morality, and justice. Under the influence of Christianity, Perkunas was transformed into the Lord of Heaven. Velnias was the guardian of wizards and sages. The goddess of forests was Medeina, and Zvorune was the goddess of hunting. There were female deities representing the sun, the moon, water, earth, and fertility. Other goddesses were responsible for the birth, life, and death of man, flora, and fauna. These deities took care that the continuity of life in the world should be maintained through the perpetual ebb and flow of life and death.

down sacred oak trees in an attempt to suppress Lithuanians' pagan (non-Christian) beliefs. Lithuanians have retained a reverence for nature and a belief in the sanctity of all living things, and elements of the ancient religion survive to this day through legends, folktales, exorcisms, and songs.

The prehistoric hunters and farmers of Lithuania had a matriarchal tribal system, and their religious imagery was female. The later patriarchal tribal and feudal systems enabled the introduction of male gods and saw the decline of the importance of goddesses, although some goddesses remained in the Lithuanian pantheon of gods side-by-side with male deities.

Places of worship were outdoors, usually in a sacred grove of trees, on a hillside, or near a holy stream. There were special people, usually men, who performed religious rituals. These men, similar to priests, were the wise men and leaders of a community. Sacrifice of animals—calves, pigs, sheep, goats, and chickens—was common and continued into the 1500s. Human sacrifice was not practiced except after a victorious battle, when the commander of the enemy forces would be sacrificed to thank the gods.

The ancient Lithuanians had a strong belief in the afterworld. The dead were buried with household objects and food for the afterlife, and warriors and leaders were buried with their horses. Grand Duke Algirdas, for example, was cremated in 1377 together with 18 horses.

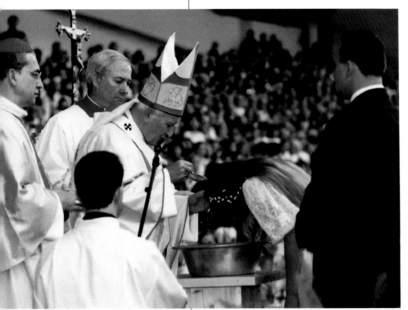

The sacrament of baptism being given to a young woman by a Catholic bishop.

CHRISTIANITY'S RUGGED ROAD

Christian teachings first reached Lithuania in the 11th and 12th centuries, but it took a long while before they were accepted. In 1251 Mindaugas adopted Christianity in his bid to have Pope Innocent crown him king, hoping to avoid attacks by Christian warriors. Soon after, though, he reverted to his old ways and sacrificed a Christian princess to Perkunas, the god of thunder. A later attempt to introduce Catholicism was more successful: Grand Duke Jogaila converted to Roman Catholicism and made it the religion of his country in 1385 when he married Princess Jadwiga of Poland.

It was a difficult beginning, though. The first Christian church in Lithuania was built near Kaunas. It had a roof that sloped steeply. According to legend, the roof had not sloped when it was constructed. The god Perkunas so mightily resented the presence of a Christian church that he engulfed it in a storm, which caused the church building to sink and so increased the slope of the roof!

Protestantism—first Lutheranism and then Calvinism—came to Lithuania in the 16th century. In the 17th century, largely due to the efforts of the Jesuits, Lithuania was reclaimed by the Roman Catholics. At that time, a number of Old Believers (the Old Ritualists) settled in Lithuania, having fled from Russia to avoid persecution. Catholicism flourished in

the 17th and 18th centuries. Many churches and monasteries were built, and the ranks of priests grew.

In 1795, however, a greater part of Lithuania was annexed to Russia, and the dominion of the Roman Catholic Church was restricted. In the 19th century the Catholic Church was persecuted. Monasteries were shut down and churches were given over to the Russian Orthodox Church. From 1799 to 1915 the Russian Orthodox faith was the official religion in Lithuania, although the Lithuanians tried to remain Catholic. The most prominent figure in the struggle to uphold the Lithuanian cultural identity was Bishop Motiejus Valancius. In time, the Russian authorities had to give in, and in 1897 the ban on building Catholic churches was lifted.

Under the Lithuanian Republic (1918–40), the Roman Catholic Church regained its place as the official religion of the state. Direct ties with the Vatican were established in 1922. The Lithuanian Church Province was created in 1926 under direct subordination to the pope, and relations with the Vatican were stabilized in 1927. The state also supported other religious communities, including other Christians as well as Muslims and Jews.

Saint Anne Church in Vilnius. This 17th-century church is now a UNESCO World Heritage Site.

Above: **A classic wooden church in the Zemaitija region.**

Opposite: **One of the two Russian Orthodox monasteries in Vilnius.**

SOVIET REPRESSION

Lithuania's incorporation into the Soviet Union in June 1940 caused major losses to all churches, including, to a lesser degree, the Russian Orthodox Church and the Old Believers. All the Catholic monasteries and 690 churches were shut down, and church lands were confiscated by the state. Many surrendered churches became concert halls or museums—Saint Casimir's, in Vilnius, was turned into a Museum of Atheism. Religious literature was suppressed, and religious instruction banned. Those who attended church could find their careers in jeopardy, and their children would be excluded from higher education.

In this atmosphere of repression, religious practices were carried on secretly. For example, a group of Catholic priests regularly published the *Chronicles of the Lithuanian Catholic Church*, which informed the world about local repression and human rights violations.

The persecution of the churches came to an end in 1988. In 1990 the Act of the Restitution of the Catholic Church was proclaimed, bringing freedom of worship once more to all Lithuanians. Today about 79 percent of Lithuanians are Roman Catholic. Monasteries and convents have reopened, and workers are renovating churches. In 1989 the Catholic organization Caritas, the Lithuanian Catholic Teachers' Union, and the Catholic Action Center resumed their activities. In 1990 the Lithuanian Catholic Academy of Sciences was moved back to Lithuania from abroad.

RUSSIAN ORTHODOX CHURCH

In 1054 Christianity underwent a major east-west division into the Roman Catholic Church and the Greek Orthodox Church, which later migrated to Russia. The name of the church in Russia is the Russian Orthodox Church. The church is headed by the Patriarch of All Russia and does not recognize the pope. Members of the Orthodox church in Lithuania are almost exclusively Russians or other Slavs. Some 4 percent of the population are followers of this faith. There are 90 small parishes and 50 congregations, governed by city and national church bodies, under the jurisdiction of the patriarchate in Moscow.

THE OLD BELIEVERS

There are 57 religious congregations headed by the Supreme Pomorski Old Ritualists' Council in Vilnius. The Old Believers is a group that formed as the result of a schism in the Russian Orthodox Church in the 17th century. Many adherents emigrated to the Baltic states, where they found more religious freedom. They have no priests and no sacraments except baptism. Since 1971, they have been officially recognized by the council of the Russian Orthodox Church.

Young Lithuanians in a cheerful procession at the Hill of Crosses near Siauliai.

OTHER CHRISTIAN DENOMINATIONS

Lutheranism came to Lithuania in the early 1500s. Today there are an estimated 20,000 members of the Lutheran Church there. There are 54 Lutheran congregations governed by the Consistory of the Evangelical Lutheran Church of Lithuania in Taurage, which has been a member of the Lutheran World Foundation since 1968. Together with the Reformed Evangelical Church, it publishes the periodical *Lietuvos evangeliku kelias* (*The Road of the Lithuanian Evangelicals*).

Other Christian denominations in Lithuania include the Reformed Evangelical Church, the Evangelical Baptists, the Evangelical Faith in the Spirit of Apostles, the Seventh-day Adventists, Calvinists, and the Eastern Rites Roman Catholics. The Reformed Evangelical Church has about 7,000 members in 14 congregations. The Lutherans, Calvinists, and Evangelists are most heavily concentrated in the coastal region, mainly because of the strong German influence in that area.

ISLAM

Islam came to Lithuania in the 14th century from the Crimea and Kazan, a town on the Volga River, through the Tatars.

For the last six centuries, the Tatars of Lithuania have maintained their ethnic identity as well as their religion. They live primarily in compact communities where the mosque is the central focus of their lives.

There were altogether 48 mosques in the grand duchy of Lithuania from 1397 to the end of the 18th century. During the commemoration in 1930 of the 500th anniversary of Vytautas the Great's death, the government of Lithuania built a mosque in Kaunas in recognition of the Tatars.

During the 50 years of Soviet occupation, Lithuanian Muslims, like other ethnic religious groups, were prevented from practicing their faith. Now about 3,235 Tatars live in Lithuania, and the Muslim community numbers about 2,860. There are five major congregations of Muslims in Lithuania, and they worship at the Raiziai Mosque in Alytus (built in the late 19th century), the Vytautas Didysis Mosque at Kaunas (1930), the Nemezis Mosque (early 20th century), and the oldest existing mosque, which is in the village of Keturiasdesimt Totoriu (1815). The lifting of religious repression since independence has cleared the way for new mosques to be built. The Tatar community is now trying to rebuild the Lukiskes Mosque in Vilnius, destroyed during the Soviet occupation.

Muslim Tatars gather at a mosque in the Vilnius region.

CROSSES AND MINIATURE CHAPELS

Crosses, chapels, and wooden carvings are traditionally erected as memorials at places where people have died. A modern adaptation of this practice can be found in the wooden carvings at Ablinga, a village that was burned with all its inhabitants by the Nazis.

As Christianity is the dominant religion in Lithuania, the image of the cross plays an important role in the life of Lithuanians. Many crosses and miniature chapels are found on posts along roadsides, in yards and on homes, on farmsteads, in graveyards, on hill slopes and hilltops, beside rivers and springs, near forests, and in town squares. Some crosses incorporate pre-Christian religious elements, such as the sun, moon, and serpents. The crosses in Lithuania can be divided into two broad types: the pillar type, which has a concealed and scarcely noticeable crossbeam, and the cross-shaped type.

Crosses are built for various purposes. Some are erected in cemeteries and in places where accidents have occurred in remembrance of the dead. They are put up in villages, fields, and along roads in the hope that God will give blessings, grant a good harvest, and keep away epidemics, droughts, quarrels, and other misfortunes. Other occasions for installing crosses include moving to a new home or farm, births, christenings, weddings, and times of success or misfortune in the family.

Miniature chapels are suspended from trees, nailed to homes, mounted on niches cut in tree trunks, or mounted on poles in fields and forests. Some are simple and others ornate. They are like miniature houses or little chapels showing a statue or statues within. In some areas it is customary to affix a chapel to a tree when there is a birth or a death in the family.

Crosses and miniature chapels are found at places that are believed to be haunted and at springs whose waters are thought to have healing powers. Miniature chapels dedicated to Saint John the Baptist are erected near rivers and bridges. Village communities, small towns, religious fraternities, and youth organizations each have their own cross.

The variety of crosses is evident in the exceptionally rich ornamentation and mix of materials. Huge crosses, some reaching 10 feet (3 m) in height, are carved out of stone. Wooden crosses and miniature chapels have ornate iron decorations that incorporate smaller crosses, trumpeting angels, and other Christian symbols into designs of radiating wavy sunbeams, arrows, crescents, stylized pine trees, lilies, and tulips.

The best example of Lithuanian crosses is the Hill of Crosses, just north of Siauliai, where thousands of crosses are mounted on a hill. The hill is not as tall as it once was. It was bulldozed by the Soviets three times, and each time new crosses would be brought to replace the demolished ones.

The Hill of Crosses near the city of Siauliai.

UŽUPIO
RES PUBLIKA

LANGUAGE

THE LITHUANIAN LANGUAGE BELONGS to the family of Indo-European languages. It is the oldest living language in Europe today and retains many archaic features. It uses the Latin alphabet with variations for special sounds. Lithuanian is spoken by some 3 million people in Lithuania and by another one million living abroad. Lithuania is also rich in dialects and regional accents. The two principal dialects are Aukstaitian (Highland Lithuanian) and Samogitian (Lowland Lithuanian). Standard Lithuanian is based on Western Aukstaitian. Other languages spoken in Lithuania include Russian (as the second language), Latvian, Polish, and Belorussian. The languages of commerce and business are English, German, and French, with English slowly gaining popularity as the favored second language.

Opposite: **A road sign in Lithuanian in Vilnius.**

Below: **Public telephone kiosks dot the streets of Vilnius.**

THE LITHUANIAN LANGUAGE

The Lithuanian language belongs to the Baltic branch of the great Indo-European family. It is related to most of the other languages of Europe and Western Asia, from India to Iceland. Its ultimate source is the extinct language of India called Sanskrit. The early Indo-European languages were spoken 5,000 years ago by people who settled in Ukraine, southern Russia, the Euphrates, the Rhine and Indus valleys, and around the Aral Sea.

The Baltic branch consists of Lithuanian, Latvian, the extinct Old Prussian language, and the extinct dialects of the Curonians, Semigallians, and Selonians. The Lithuanian and Latvian languages separated during the fifth to seventh centuries A.D., with Lithuanian retaining more ancient features than Latvian.

Of all the living languages in Europe today, Lithuanian is the most archaic and has most faithfully preserved the primitive features of Sanskrit.

A bookseller in Vilna, Lithuania, in 1914, displaying her books for sale in baskets.

This has happened because Lithuanian was spoken by a people whose environment isolated them for many centuries from the outside world by dense forests and impassable marshes.

A very great many Lithuanian words are used by Belorussians and Poles in the areas formerly inhabited by Lithuanians. A complete dictionary of the Lithuanian language consists of 20 volumes, containing about 400,000 entries.

During the Soviet era, Russian increasingly displaced Lithuanian in the country's cultural, economic, administrative, and political life. Major government institutions operated entirely in Russian. In 1989 the government reinstated Lithuanian as the national language. During the Soviet times, Lithuanian was written in their Cyrillic script, but after independence was proclaimed in 1990, the Lithuanian language reverted to the Latin alphabet.

Teaching Lithuanian language and literature was prohibited from 1861 to 1904, and again from 1940 to 1989.

PRONUNCIATION GUIDE

The Lithuanian language uses the Latin alphabet. There are 32 letters in the alphabet. Unique Lithuanian sounds are represented by special characters.

Vowels

a – as in *a*h	e – as in there	ė – as in make	i – as in s*i*t
o – as in sh*o*t	u – as in should	ū– oo as in truth	y – ee as in s*ee*

ą, ę, į, ų appear in special cases and are pronounced a bit longer.

Consonants: b, d, f, g, h, k, l, m, n, p, t, and v are pronounced almost as in English

c – ts as in tickets	č – ch as in chin	s – as in sit	š – sh as in s*h*e
z – as in *z*oo	ž –as in vision	j – y as in *y*es	r – is always trilled

LITHUANIAN WISDOM AND ADVICE

Every nation has its treasury of proverbs, brief and popular statements of wisdom or advice. Called *patarle* (PAH-tehr-lay) in Lithuanian, proverbs are easy to remember.

In traveling globally by word of mouth from person to person, proverbs often retain their deeper meaning but change in their manner of expression according to local circumstances. Thus the English proverb "A bird in the hand is worth two in the bush" appears in Lithuanian as "A sparrow in the hand is better than an elk in the woods" and "A sparrow in the palm is better than a crane on the roof."

Traditional wisdom, proverbs, riddles, folk tales, and gossip are passed on through word of mouth.

Sometimes Lithuanians copied proverbs exactly, like the Sanskrit proverb "God has given teeth, God will give bread." At other times they expressed ideas in their own way. Thus the English proverb "You can't get blood out of a stone" becomes "You can't shatter a wall with your head."

How would you describe a gluttonous and lazy person? Lithuanians would say he or she "eats like a horse and works like a rooster." How about a man who is happy for no reason? He would be said to be "as happy as though he has found a bit of iron." Such Lithuanian sayings and maxims are full of humor and are used as tools to educate children. Looking for something? "Maybe you'll find it in the dew!"

LITHUANIAN RIDDLES

Which tongue (language) is easiest for everyone?
The mother tongue.

A young lady in the bathhouse, her braids outside.
A carrot.

A dark tablecloth covered with crumbs and a chunk of bacon.
The sky, stars, and moon.

Though it bends, it breaks not.
Smoke.

It burns without fire and beats without a stick.
The heart.

Lithuanian surnames reflect both the person's sex and the marital status of the women. A husband, wife, and unmarried daughter thus all have different forms of the same name. For example, the husband's surname is Adamkus, wife is Adamkiene and daughter is Adamkute.

STORYTELLING

At parties and gatherings, storytelling is a popular form of entertainment. Popular legends are inhabited by devils, sorcerers, ghosts, and spirits. These stories are of pre-Christian origin. According to legends, people traveling in remote places and at odd hours might come across these creatures. The outcome of such encounters is sometimes happy and sometimes not.

If you find a piece of horse manure in the place of the new pipe that you bought last night, you can be sure that the traveler you traded with was no ordinary man, but a devil. If you left an infant out in the fields overnight by mistake, you might find only its bones the next morning and know that some spirits had been at work. Tame spirits were good, however, and carried riches and goods to their masters.

Short stories without endings and tales about animals are especially popular among children. Domestic and forest animals that behave like human beings inhabit these stories. Heroes are often aided by magical objects and heavenly or earthly helpers. There are also modern stories about clever hired hands, gullible landlords, and matchmakers. Often, stories are embellished with short, simple songs, as if a character in the story were singing it.

Mystical stories are common and are often the most artful. In these tales, heroes battle dragons or free people who have been turned into swans or other beings. The tragic story of Zilvinas, the king of the grass snakes, his wife Egle, and their family is a relic of the ancient cult of the grass snake.

This devilish character is one of the strange and magical creatures who inhabit the enchanted world of Lithuanian stories and legends.

EGLE, QUEEN OF THE GRASS SNAKES

Once upon a time there was an old man and an old woman. They had 12 sons and 3 daughters. The youngest daughter's name was Egle, and she was the darling of the family. One summer evening she went for a swim in the sea. When she finished her swim and wanted to change back into her clothes, she found a grass snake lying curled in her shirtsleeve. He said he would give her shirt back if she agreed to marry him. So Egle promised to marry him.

In a few days, she left her parents' house escorted by a retinue of grass snakes. On the shore of the sea she was met by a handsome young man who was actually the grass snake that had curled up in her shirtsleeve. They crossed in a boat to an island nearby, and from there they descended into a beautiful palace at the bottom of the sea where they celebrated their wedding. Life in the palace was blissful. Egle forgot her homeland altogether, for she was happy. She gave birth to three sons—Azuolas (Oak), Uosis (Ash), and Berzas (Birch)—and last, a daughter, Drebule (Aspen).

Nine years passed. Her oldest son asked her where her parents were and said he would like to visit them. Egle remembered her family again and wanted to go to see them, but her husband, Zilvinas, would not let her go because he was afraid she would not come back. He asked her to finish three tasks before she would be allowed to go.

The first task was to spin a bundle of silk. Egle spun and spun, but no matter how fast she worked, the bundle stayed the same size, so she asked a wise old woman for advice. The woman told her to throw the bundle into the fire. The unspun silk burned away to reveal a toad that had been producing new silk as Egle spun. Her second task was to wear down iron shoes. Egle accomplished this task also with the advice of the old woman, who told her to go to a foundry and ask the blacksmith to burn them down. Her third task was to bake a pie with just a sieve for a tool. But Zilvinas had given orders to hide all the water-holding and cooking vessels in the kingdom. Egle could not even fetch water for the pie. On the advice of the old woman, she filled the holes of the sieve with bread dough, let it dry, and then brought some water from the river in it and made the pie.

Having accomplished all three tasks, she said good-bye to her husband on the seashore and, together with her children, departed for her parents' house. Before parting, Egle agreed that when she came back she would call her husband out of the sea by saying "Zilvinas, Zilvinas, if alive you are, milk white is the surf! If dead you are, bloodred is the surf!"

Egle and her children had a very good time with her parents and siblings. When the time allotted for the visit was drawing to a close, Egle's brothers were unhappy and tried to get the password from her sons, so they could go and kill Zilvinas. Try as they would, they could not get it out of her sons. But the daughter, Aspen, blurted it out when her uncles threatened to flog her.

When Egle and her children came back to the seashore and tried to call Zilvinas, they found the roiling surf breaking bloodred on the shore, and heard Zilvinas's voice coming from the bottom of the sea telling them of the betrayal. In her grief and pain, Egle turned her sons into strong trees—oak, ash, and birch. She turned her daughter into the quivering aspen and herself into the fir tree.

ARTS

THE ARTS AND CULTURAL SCENE in Lithuania is lively. Theaters, concert halls, museums, and exhibition halls are open year-round. During the summer months, many cultural festivals and drama and music competitions are held. There are many professional theaters, some state orchestras, and chamber groups in the major cities. Lithuania also has as many as 53 museums, with the Mykolas Zilinskas gallery in Kaunas holding the most significant collection of works of art.

THEATER AND BALLET

Lithuania has a very long history of performance art, arising from ancient rituals and entertainments.

During the Soviet era, several Lithuanian plays were banned, and the theater had to extol the virtues of Communism. Now that Lithuania is independent again, the theater enjoys much more freedom. In Vilnius, there are 13 professional theaters and a number of concert halls. Kaunas has a branch of the National Philharmonic Orchestra, a pantomime theater school, a puppet theater, and a youth chamber music theater. The Lithuanian Theater of Youth is popular locally and is known abroad.

Lithuanian ballet has a reputation of high professional quality. At the outset of World War II, many fine dancers fled the country. After the war, however, the Academic Opera and Ballet Theater revived and continued to operate in Vilnius even throughout the Soviet years. It performed several Lithuanian pieces, and elements of folk dancing were skillfully worked into its repertoire. Today, the ballet company is 68 dancers strong. Some of its soloists, such as Egle Spokaite and Ruta Jezerskyte, have won many prizes in international competitions.

Above: **This ballerina is Svetlana Beriosova (1932–98), a Lithuanian who achieved international fame.**

Opposite: **A powerful sculpture of the three muses rises above the entrance to the Academic Drama Theater in Vilnius.**

93

MUSIC FESTIVALS

March	Jazz festival, Birstonas
April	Jauna electronic and electroacoustic festival, Vilnius
	Jazz festival, Kaunas
May	Youth chamber music, Druskininkai
	Skamba (*skamba kankliai*) folk music festival, Vilnius
August	Pop music festival, Palanga
September	Griezyne folk music festival, Vilnius International pop music festival, Vilnius Fall Grok Jurgeli, folk music festival, Kaunas
October	Jazz festival, Vilnius Gaida Baltica contemporary music festival, Gaida
November	Italian opera week
	Is Arti contemporary music festival, Kaunas
Every three years	Baltica Folklore Festival
Every five years	Dainu Svente, traditional choral festival (There are many national choral song festivals to watch for in the country.)

Lithuanians of all ages enjoy coming together to sing.

MUSIC

The Baltic states are famous for their choral singing. So far, about 500,000 Lithuanian folk songs have been collated, including songs about work, love, war, and motherhood. There are many professional and amateur choirs in Lithuania. Every five years there is a huge song festival called Dainu Svente, where choirs, folk dance ensembles, and folk orchestras come from all over Lithuania to perform. Choir members number in the thousands and the audiences in tens or even hundreds of thousands—a large proportion of the population. There are also smaller song and dance festivals throughout the year. Under Soviet rule, these festivals were among the very few ways in which national feeling could be legally expressed, although several of the more ardent patriotic songs were banned. The song festivals became a vehicle for nationalist sentiment, and the independence movement in the Baltic states has often been called the Singing Revolution.

Lithuania has produced several notable composers, including M. K. Ciurlionis and modernist Osvaldas Balakauskas. Onute Narbutaite is the most famous Lithuanian composer today. The National Philharmonic building in Vilnius houses the symphony orchestra and is also an umbrella organization for many other musical groups and soloists. There is an

active live music scene, with bands performing rock, alternative music, and jazz throughout the land.

Artists played an important leadership role in the Baltic independence movement. In Lithuania, a music professor, Vytautas Landsbergis, became the country's leader in 1990. Popular culture—particularly rock music, which was banned under Soviet rule—united many sections of the population and was used to express defiance during the 1980s. The most influential rock group in the 1980s was Foje, whose gloomy lyrics were reflective of life under Soviet rule. Although rock music today has not reached the dizzying heights it did two decades ago, it is still as popular. This is evident in the increase in the number of rock festivals in major cities.

FOLK ART

Lithuanian folk art embraces a great variety of forms from graphic art, religious art, and primitive painting to woodcarving, textiles, ceramics, and blacksmithing. Folk craft festivals and displays are a popular feature of Lithuania's cultural life.

Lithuania has an especially rich tradition of woodcarving. One ancient craft was the carving of ritual wooden masks. These carvings have preserved some elements of ancient sorcery practices. Their most distinctive feature is folk humor and satire. Wooden crosses are another important folk art. They are often covered with ancient pre-Christian symbols. A more modern example of Lithuanian woodcarving skill is the group of wooden memorial sculptures commemorating the residents of the village of Ablinga, which was burned together with all its inhabitants by the Nazis. In the field where Ablinga once stood, about 25 miles (40 km) from Klaipeda, large wooden sculptures have been erected for the families of the dead. Sculptures made from flax and straw are also popular. Elaborate sculptures like the "wedding gardens" are particularly enjoyed in Aukstaitija. Other well-known examples of folk arts can be seen at the Witches' Hill in Juodkrante and at the Hill of Crosses near Siauliai.

Above: **The weaving of sashes is a traditional skill that is passed from mother to daughter as part of the daughter's coming-of-age rituals.**

Opposite: **Painted in 1903, this work by M.K. Ciurlionis is from the "Funeral" cycle. Ciurlionis was a mystic who saw nature as an inexhaustible source of beauty.**

TWO LITHUANIAN ARTISTS

M. K. CIURLIONIS Mikalojus Konstantinas Ciurlionis (1875–1911) was born in the Dzukija region. Before he died, at the early age of 36, he almost single-handedly founded modern Lithuanian culture through his work as a painter, composer, and organizer of cultural events.

Both in painting and music, Ciurlionis was a pioneer and founder of new forms. He composed many works that are still performed, including the first Lithuanian symphony, *In the Forest*.

After establishing himself as a composer, Ciurlionis took up painting, believing that there were certain emotions that were better

expressed in shapes and colors than in music. In his painting he created a mystical universe with motifs from Lithuanian folklore. He was among those who initiated the annual Lithuanian Art Exhibition in Vilnius in 1907.

PETRAS KALPOKAS (1880–1945) The works of this Lithuanian artist belong to the period of the formation of Lithuania's national fine arts awareness. He took deep interest in the first Lithuanian Art Exhibition in 1907 and was an active participant in other art exhibitions. He engaged in various fields of art, producing paintings, frescos, and cartoons. His major works, however, were landscape and portrait paintings. He taught painting at the Kaunas School of Art and at the Institute of Decorative and Applied Arts.

Other artists in Lithuania include Sarunas Sauka, a noted postmodernist painter, and Vygantas Paukšte, regarded as the father of Lithuanian postmodernism.

A tribute of flowers before a statue of the poet Salomeja Neris.

LITERATURE

Lithuania's first pieces of writing date back to the Middle Ages. They were not written in Lithuanian, however, but in Old Church Slavic, Latin, and Polish.

The first book in the Lithuanian language, the Protestant Catechism, was printed in 1547. The Lithuanian text, in Gothic letters, is often uneven and not clearly printed. When out of one type, the printer simply substituted it with another! Between 200 and 300 copies were printed. Only two copies remain today—one in the library of Vilnius University and the other in the library of Torun University, Poland.

During the next two centuries, more religious texts in the local language appeared as more people learned to read. This laid the foundation for Lithuania's literary language.

Several Lithuanian writers wrote patriotic ballads and prose during the 18th century Russian occupation. In 1864 the Russian czar banned the printing of Lithuanian works. Poetic literature flourished across the border in Prussia, however, where the Lithuanian poet Maironis lived, and in the émigré community in the United States. Maironis was a leader in glorifying all things Lithuanian. His verses are still read, and his poems have been translated into English. Some of the leading poets of the period include Vilius Vydunas, Juozas Tumas-Vaizgantas, and Antanas Vienuolis. Prose writing developed after the ban was lifted in 1904.

Independence in 1918 ushered in a new era of creativity. Vincas Mykolaitis-Putinas wrote *Altoriu Sesely*, one of Lithuania's major novels.

FROM BIRUTE MOUNTAIN

Rolling wind-driven breakers ashore from the West,
Splash my breast with the chill of your waves, or to me
Grant your power, with such strength my spirit invest
That I speak just as grandly as you, Baltic Sea!

How I longed for you, infinite one! How I yearned
Just to hear your mysterious voice again!
You alone can appreciate me, you who scorned
Through the ages your towering waves to restrain!

Are you sad? So am I! And I do not know why;
It's my wish that the storm should howl louder for me:
Though it offers no tranquil forgetfulness, I
Always strive to be closer to you, Baltic Sea!

And I wish for a friend who will help me to face
All the storms of my heart and will soothe my heart's pain,
Who shall not by a dark look my secret betray
But restless as I am, shall ever remain.

—*Maironis (1895), translated by Lionginas Pazusis*

Women writers, such as Žemait (Julija Zymantiene), Sofija Ciurlioniene, and the poet Salomeja Neris, flourished.

Although some good prose and poetry were produced during the Soviet era, the repression stifled literary development overall. Often the writings in the 1990s reflect the writers' experience of the Soviet occupation, and many express a dark, cynical, and sad tone. Popular writers include Juozas Aputis, Vytautas Bubnys, and Vytautas Martinkus. The novels of Bubnys and Martinkus show the continuing attraction of folk themes.

Two internationally known contemporary writers of the Lithuanian language are the poet and essayist Tomas Venclova, and satirist and children's author Vytaute Zilinskaite. The Lithuanian Writers' Union also helped advance the literary scene by offering contemporary Lithuanian poetry and prose in its English language magazine, *Vilnius*.

The Lithuanian Chronicles, *written in Old Church Slavic in the 1400s, relate Lithuanian legends, such as the founding of Vilnius, and stories of heroes and heroines.*

The architecture of Trakai castle mixes early Gothic style with local touches.

ARCHITECTURE

Lithuania's rural architecture expresses the people's farming background and lifestyle. Timber is by far the most common building material. The earliest houses had thatched roofs; later, wood shingles, clay, and tin were used. Some buildings have ornately carved woodwork. The skills of building are passed along from generation to generation with few changes introduced along the way. The oldest standing wooden houses date back to the 18th century.

City architecture—fortifications and churches—was of stone, and it is these buildings that give the old cities their stable atmosphere today. Other buildings were made of wood until the 19th century.

Architectural styles followed those of western Europe. Early Gothic structures in Lithuania were heavy, massive buildings with thick walls, small windows, and huge, imposing buttresses. Examples of typical early Gothic architecture in the country are Saint Michael's Church in Vilnius, built at the end of the 14th century, and Saint Michael's Church in Kaunas. Late Gothic churches of the 15th and 16th centuries are much larger and lighter structures. The best example of this progression is Saint Anne's Church in Vilnius.

The high baroque period produced the Church of Saints Peter and Paul in Vilnius and the church and convent of the Sisters of Saint Casimir at Pazaislis near Kaunas. The convent is hexagonal and had a great copper roof. Over the centuries it has suffered from the vandalism and looting of invading armies.

In the late 18th century, classicism and romanticism became the predominant architectural styles. Towns followed a rectangular grid. During the 19th century many of the cities' wooden buildings were replaced with stone structures.

After independence in 1918, an intensive growth of towns began. The countryside changed radically as the land was divided into individual holdings spreading all over the country. Rural architecture continued to maintain the traditions of Lithuanian folk architecture.

Architecture took a step backward during the Soviet era. Huge, drab, jerry-built high-rises and housing projects were the buildings of the day. Many are already dilapidated. Today, the restoration of these existing buildings takes precedence over undertaking any brand-new housing projects.

Tourists file along the upper balconies of a 15th-century castle that has been restored and is now a museum.

LEISURE

WINTERS ARE LONG AND COLD, and summers are very short in Lithuania. During the winter months, indoor leisure activities are popular, especially storytelling by grandparents. Woodcarving and handicrafts created from flax and fibers are old traditions for occupying the short winter days, as is singing and playing of musical instruments. Other pastimes popular in the winter are skiing and ice skating.

During the summer, Lithuanians make the most of the warm weather. Forests, rivers, and lakes are within easy reach of city and country alike. In June, when the school term ends, many children are sent to stay with relatives in the country for the entire three-month vacation. Their mothers may accompany them, and fathers visit on weekends.

In the country there is less leisure time than in the city. Leisure time is generally used for handicrafts. Women's and girls' hobbies include drawing, knitting, crocheting, and sash weaving. These skills are passed down from mother to daughter. There are also get-togethers for name days and other church and traditional holidays, weddings, christenings, funerals, and even for the slaughter of an animal, when neighbors and relatives are invited for a feast.

Young people from the country go to nearby towns to see plays, visit dance clubs, or play sports. The most popular sport in Lithuania is basketball. In bad weather, young city people gather in cafés to talk, listen to music, use the Internet, and drink coffee. Most cafés also serve alcohol. Vilnius specializes in beer bars, which are often cavernous cellars.

Above: **Lithuanians resting beside a quiet stream in the country.**

Opposite: **Families enjoy relaxing along a beach on the Baltic coast in Palanga.**

TENDING THE GARDEN

Lithuanians like growing things—vegetables in their backyards, and flowers and herbs on their balconies and windowsills. They are never more than a few generations from their farmer roots, and almost all maintain some kind of tie to the land. Most urban people own garden plots on the outskirts of the cities and towns. Restrictions limiting buildings on these plots have become unenforceable, and summer houses have become more and more substantial. About 14 percent of state land is used for garden plots by urban dwellers and educational establishments. In spring, summer, and early fall, families or groups of friends go to the plots on weekends to tend the gardens and fruit trees or just to relax. Older people who no longer have to worry about jobs just move out to their place for the summer.

SINGING

Singing is a way of life in Lithuania. Family get-togethers are occasions to sit and sing songs of their ancient land, mythology, customs, and folklore. Lithuanians are good at improvisation, and they even make up lullabies.

People young and old join song and dance groups, traditional country bands, or pop groups to occupy their leisure hours. The many music festivals held throughout Lithuania are testament to the people's love of singing. Some of the songs are about the sun, moon, and stars, and songs about magical transformations abound. In songs about orphans, the moon is often asked to become the orphan's father and the sun to become the mother. A dead father sometimes reappears transformed into an oak tree. Other songs are about Lithuanian history and social commentary and protest. There are songs for dances and games, humorous and satirical songs, and songs about family life.

MOVIES

A popular way of spending an evening is to watch a film at the local movie theater, found in many Lithuanian towns. Some of the movies are dubbed in Lithuanian, while others are shown in the original language with Lithuanian subtitles. Major U.S. and European productions are usually shown. There is also a small local movie industry; however, new film projects have been few due to a lack of funds. Well-known American film directors Jonas Mekas and Robert Zemeckis are both of Lithuanian descent.

Choral singing is a very popular activity. Most towns have a choir, many of them attaining professional standards.

SPORTS

The most favored individual sports are noncompetitive. Swimming is extremely popular, especially in rivers and lakes. Beach resorts are also well liked, especially the one at Palanga.

Fishing is a favorite pastime, too, and there are abundant fish in the thousands of lakes and rivers of Lithuania. When the lakes are frozen solid, ice fishing is practiced. A well-known spot for ice fishing is the Curonian Lagoon. Hang gliding is common in the town of Prienai, where gliders are produced. Ice skating, skiing, and tobogganing have long been popular among young Lithuanians too.

Competitive sports are basketball, volleyball, and soccer. Hands down, the most popular is basketball, and every Lithuanian boy's hero is the great player Arvydas Sabonis, who played for the Portland Trail Blazers in the United States from 1995 to 2003.

Many Lithuanians are also regular participants in activities organized by sports clubs. There are more than 800 sports clubs, including ones for weightlifting, wrestling, judo, and tennis. Young people particularly enjoy cycling and badminton.

At the 2000 Sydney Olympics, Lithuania won gold medals for trap shooting and discus throw. Lithuania's Virgilijus Alekna claimed gold again for the discus throw in 2004 in Athens.

106

STEPONAS DARIUS

The game at which Lithuanians excel is basketball. During the Soviet era, Lithuania provided the best players for the Soviet team, and the Kaunas team won the Soviet championship twice. The basketball team took home the gold in the Europe Championship in 1937, 1939, and 2003. In 1992, 1996, and 2000, the national team won the bronze medal at the Summer Olympics, and came in fourth in 2004.

The history of basketball in Lithuania begins with one of the country's great heroes, Steponas Darius. He was born in 1896. In 1907 his family emigrated to the United States, where he excelled at baseball, football, and basketball. He fought in France during World War I and returned to the United States with two decorations.

In 1920 he was one of the U.S. volunteers who took part in the liberation of occupied Lithuania. He stayed in Lithuania for seven years. During that time, he introduced basketball to the country and became a champion sportsman.

After his return to the United States in 1927, he worked in civil aviation and founded a Lithuanian flying club, Vytis. Five years later, he and his colleague Stasys Girenas set out to bring fame and glory to their newly independent nation by embarking on an epic flight from New York to Lithuania. They scraped together enough money to buy an old plane, which they called the *Lituanica*.

The plane took off from New York on July 15, 1933, and flew across the Atlantic in 37 hours 11 minutes, but it never arrived in Lithuania. No one knows why, but the plane crashed in Germany. Rumors that the *Lituanica* had been deliberately brought down by the Germans did not improve international relations. Their bodies were taken to Kaunas, then the provisional capital, where 60,000 people attended their funeral.

Despite its tragic end, many felt that the flight had put Lithuania on the map. The duo's portraits appeared on postage stamps, coins, and medals, and numerous streets, bridges, and schools were named after them. In 2001 their portrait on the LTL10 banknote honored the duo.

Monuments have been erected in their memory in Chicago in the United States, Lithuania, and Poland. One of the most popular monuments to the heroes is near Anyksciai on a huge boulder called Puntukas. This ancient landmark is one of the country's mythical stones. In 1943 a Lithuanian sculptor was in the countryside, hiding from the Germans, and he made a shelter beside the boulder. To while away the time, he carved a relief of the faces of the two pilots into the stone, adding the text of their will, which had been written before they embarked on their historic flight.

TOURING

Hikers of all ages walk throughout Lithuania, visiting historical and religious sites. Battle sites are particularly popular. At these areas, people often stop to learn folk and patriotic songs.

During the summer, Lithuanians travel over their picturesque country by bike, foot, and car, and on the waterways by canoe, raft, and boat. Along the way they visit history and craft museums, towns, cities, settlements, and farmsteads, national parks, ancient places of worship, forests, hills, and lakes. Birders often frequent the west coast, in particular the town of Vente to the east of the Curonian Lagoon, where large numbers of birds may be seen. Huge boulders are another attraction. One boulder is 75 feet (23 m) long, 21 feet (6.5 m) wide, and 13 feet (4 m) high.

Hikers resting at the top of a climb to view this stunning scene.

SAUNAS AND ICE BATHS

Enjoying saunas is a popular leisure activity. Lithuanians love the alternate hot and cold sensations that a sauna and their country's climate provide. Saunas are built near streams or lakes, so that after a session in a steamy sauna, a bather can plunge into the icy waters next to it.

In the wintertime, a large number of Lithuanians take dips in "ice holes." Some even bravely swim in the Baltic Sea among the ice floes.

The town of Druskininkai, on the Nemunas River, is famous for its mineral springs and therapeutic mud, well-equipped sanatoriums, comfortable holiday homes, parks, beautiful surroundings, and pleasant climate. This health resort, situated 87 miles (140 km) from Vilnius, attracts some 400,000 visitors a year.

Ice fishing through holes cut on a frozen lake near Siauliai.

Dancing in traditional dress during a festival.

DANCING AND GAMES

For Lithuanians, ballroom dances are more popular than games. Ballroom dancing became popular at the beginning of the 20th century. Today, the Austrian waltz, Hungarian Vengerka, Spanish Padespan, Polish Krakowiak, and Russian Kokietka are danced in villages and cities alike. The French square dance and the Bohemian polka are very popular in villages. Lithuanian quadrilles, the *šustas* (SHOOS-tahs), *jonkelis* (YONG-kay-lis), and *žekelis* (ZHAY-kay-lis) all developed under Swedish influence.

In 1911 Matas Grigonis published a collection of 200 games. Formerly, games did not differ from simple folk dances—both are based on singing and dancing. Games have retained singing throughout the years, whereas dances became more complicated and lively, until eventually instrumental music replaced singing.

Walking in a single or double circle, a half circle, or in rows is characteristic of games. The movements of players follow the rhythm of the song, becoming slower or faster along with the song. Movements consist of clapping, turning, bending, and "passing through." In games, there is no limit to the number of participants. These types of games are rather old-fashioned today, and they are most often played as demonstrations of a bygone art.

CLAY WHISTLES AND BIRDHOUSES

Clay whistles are popular, and adults make them for their children in an astonishing array of shapes and forms. Lithuanian children are particularly fond of clay whistles made in the shapes of horses, riders, and lambs for the boys, and ducklings, birds, and flowers for the girls.

In springtime, young and old alike occupy themselves making birdhouses. These are mounted on poles near homes to welcome the returning summer visitors—jackdaws, starlings, and others. Old wagon wheels are put on roofs or on tall trees to attract the returning storks looking for building sites for their sturdy nests.

EASY PICKINGS

Lithuanians are fond of picking mushrooms in the forests, where there are over 100 varieties of edible mushrooms. People also go out during the summer and fall to pick wild strawberries, blueberries, raspberries, lingonberries, and cranberries.

Children make their own whistles from willow bark. Most young boys in Lithuania can make and play small *birbynes* (beer-BEE-nus), or reed-pipes, and *lamzdelis* (lum-zhe-DAY-lis), similar to a recorder made out of wood or thick bark.

FESTIVALS

THE SPIRIT OF LITHUANIAN FESTIVALS has been kept alive through the years by strong family ties and the commitment of country people to their traditions. Lithuanian festivals are fostered by the many ethnic cultural centers, clubs, folklore ensembles, and places of worship.

Today religious and seasonal festivals, as well as ethnic festivals, are celebrated all over Lithuania. Sometimes elements of all types show up in a favorite festival.

There are more than 500 youth and adult folkloric groups in Lithuania. Student ensembles, from secondary schools to universities, are very active in performing at Lithuania's festivals. The first time a song festival took place was in Kaunas in 1924. At that event, only 86 choral groups and 3,000 singers took part. Today, this popular festival brings in hundreds and even thousands of performers.

Left: **The pre-Christian festivals are based on the cycle of the seasons and crops. These celebrants are observing the festival of the spring equinox on March 21, when day and night are exactly the same length.**

Opposite: **Men wearing classic attire lighting a traditional bonfire on Midsummer Day in Kernave. This is known as the feast of Saint John.**

LITHUANIAN HOLIDAYS

January 1*	New Year's Day
January 6	Three Kings' Day
January 13	Defenders of Freedom Day: commemorates those who were killed or wounded by Soviet troops on January 13, 1991
February 16*	Independence Day (1918)
March 4	Saint Casimir's Day: celebrates the coming of spring
March 11	Restoration of Lithuania's independence in 1990
March/April*	Easter
June 14	Day of Mourning and Hope: anniversary of the first mass deportation of Lithuanians to Siberia in 1941
July 6*	Statehood Day: coronation of Mindaugas in 1253
August 15	Feast of the Assumption
August 23	Black Ribbon Day: signing of a secret pact between Hitler and Stalin to divide up the Baltic states (1939)
September 8	Nation Day: birth of the Virgin Mary and the coronation of Vytautas the Great in 1430
November 1*	All Saints' Day
November 23	Lithuanian Soldiers' Day
December 25, 26*	Christmas Day and Boxing Day

*Official public holidays

MIDSUMMER DAY

Saint John the Baptist's Day falls on June 24, which is Midsummer Day in the pre-Christian tradition. When Catholicism arrived in Lithuania, the Church incorporated this major holiday into Christian activities by combining it with the popular saint's day, but many ancient traditions still predominate in modern celebrations of midsummer.

Most of the festivities take place on the eve of the holiday. Girls and women gather flowers and herbs, which are believed to heal illnesses if collected at this time. These are woven into wreaths and either worn on the head or cast adrift in streams and rivers. People light bonfires and sing and dance around them, jump over them, and play games. The glow from the bonfires can be seen from afar, spreading light over crops, thus ensuring protection from harm. The flames are believed to have cleansing and healing powers. Weeds from the fields are pulled up and thrown into the fires. Later, the ashes are spread on the fields. At home the hearth fire is extinguished and then rekindled with embers from the bonfire.

HARVEST FESTIVALS

Ancient Lithuanians' celebrations fell on the most significant days of the year: the solstices, equinoxes, and harvests. Since Lithuania is primarily an agricultural nation, it is not surprising that many festivals are connected with farming and animal husbandry.

Celebrating the rye harvest festival in characteristic rustic style.

There are many traditional festivities associated with the rye harvest. When the rye harvest begins, the first plants gathered are tied into a small sheaf. This bundle is called the Diedas (old man) or the Guest, and is set up behind the table in the place of honor. It stands there as a symbol of plenty.

Before the main harvest, the family gathers with neighboring families at the far end of their fields to divide a loaf of rye bread together, saying, "Bread meets bread" as they eat it.

The reapers leave a small patch of rye stalks growing on the field at the end of the harvest. When they have finished, they stand in a circle around this clump, cover their hands with scarves or aprons, and uproot any weeds from between the stalks. These stalks are then braided and bent toward the farmstead to ensure that wealth flows from the fields to the household.

The reapers weave a harvest wreath from the best ears of rye for the head harvester to carry to the owner of the farm. The entire group of harvesters greets the landowner, who then serves everyone a lavish harvest feast.

SHROVETIDE

Shrovetide, or Užgavenes (OO-zhe-GAH-veh-nes), is celebrated in March on Shrove Tuesday, the last day before the 40-day fast for Lent that is traditional for Catholics. The verb *uzgaveti* (OO-zhe-GAH-veh-tee) means "to eat well and heartily." This festival is full of humor, jokes, superstitions, fortune-telling, and feasting to celebrate the end of winter. It is a merry carnival, a masquerade full of pranks, with a drama performed outdoors to cast off winter and welcome spring. Elsewhere this is known as Mardi Gras or Carnival.

At dusk, men dress up in costumes with humorous, satirical, or animal masks. They go from house to house, deriding housewives or workers lagging behind in their chores. Some dress as evil spirits or demons with pitchforks. Many people dress up as traditional characters. Popular characters are Kanapinis, the Hemp Man, because during Lent hemp oil is used for light instead of tallow candles; a thief looking for something to steal; a beggar; or characters rarely seen in the village—the doctor and the soldier. Animal figures include horses, goats, and storks. Men disguise themselves as women and vice versa. An old woman, More—a symbol of the clash between winter and spring—is wheeled about in a cart. In one hand she holds a flail and in the other a broom, for she cannot make up her mind whether she should continue to flail last year's harvest or start sweeping the yard and set about the spring cleaning!

PALM SUNDAY AND EASTER

Bunches of dried grasses and flowers and small branches are sold on the street and near churches on Palm Sunday.

It is traditional to attend church on Palm Sunday morning with a bunch of juniper or pussy willow branches. At first light on Palm Sunday, family members compete to get up before the others so that the early ones can tap the sleepers with the green branches, singing: "It is not me who is flogging you, it is the Palm Sunday juniper doing it. Easter comes in a week. Do you promise me an Easter egg?" After the church service, the pretend flogging continues in the streets. This is a way of wishing each other to be as healthy as the green twigs.

On Easter morning, the floggers receive decorated Easter eggs. The hard-cooked eggs are covered with wax designs then dipped in dyes, or first given a color bath and then carved with a sharp knife or a piece of glass. The eggs are eaten on Easter morning. Children receive their eggs from the Easter Granny, who leaves eggs in a tidy nest outside the house or in a basket hanging from a tree. The children never see her, of course, for she arrives before sunrise in a little cart pulled by a wax horse (the wax horse would melt if she came after the sun had risen).

CHRISTMAS

Lithuanians celebrate Christmas Eve, or Kucios (KOO-chi-ohs), faithfully. The women scrub and decorate the house. In rural areas, the men clean the yard and prepare special fodder for the animals. When the day's work is done, everyone bathes and dresses in their best clothes. When the evening star appears, the family sits down at the table. It is important to be at home for the Christmas Eve dinner, and sometimes people will undertake long journeys to be with their families. Travelers and friends are also welcomed.

For the evening meal the table is spread with hay in memory of the birth of Christ in the manger, and covered with a white linen cloth. Plates are decorated with a fir twig or sprig of myrtle. Sometimes hay is placed under or on each plate. A Christmas Eve wafer is placed on each plate. These wafers, *kaledaiciai* (kah-le-DY-chi-eye) are made of unleavened wheat dough, and blessed in the church. A cross is placed at the center of the table. People sit down at the table in order of seniority, leaving empty spaces for absent members.

The meal begins with a prayer. Then the head of the family breaks a wafer and shares it with all at the table, extending greetings and good wishes. Everyone else then does the same.

Customarily, 12 courses are placed on the table, one for each month of the year, signifying that the family will have enough food all year. The dishes are prepared from wheat, oat, and barley flours, groats (crushed grain of various cereals), fish, mushrooms, poppy seeds, fruits, berries, honey, and hemp oil. No milk or meat is served. The meal ends with a prayer and the singing of a Christmas hymn. After the feast, both adults and children enjoy telling fortunes by drawing stalks of hay from under the tablecloth. If a girl draws a thin stalk, for example, her future husband will be tall and thin. Or if a married man pulls a plump stem, it means a prosperous year for him. On farms the hay from the table is then given to the animals.

The Christmas tree tradition came to Lithuania at the beginning of the 20th century. In 1908, pine trees were decorated on some farms in Zemaitija for the children of the laborers. In 1910 they appeared in a few schools and orphanages. After World War I the custom spread to the cities, but it took longer to reach the villages. The trees are decorated with ornaments made of straw, painted eggshells, and figures made out of pastry. These could be birds, horses, squirrels, lambs, moons, suns, stars, flowers, or

Costumed adults and children participate in a parade on January 6, Three Kings' Day.

ALL SAINTS' DAY

All Saints' Day, celebrated on November 1, is an occasion to remember and pray for the dead. On this day, as well as on November 2, All Souls' Day, Lithuanians decorate family graves with flowers, plants, and burning candles. It is thought that doing this brings the spirits nearer and helps to form a bond between the living and the dead. Since ancient times, Lithuanians have believed that after death the soul separates from the body but continues existing among the living. In some places, bread is baked and distributed to the poor. This ensures that the coming year's honey and rye harvests will be plentiful.

STORK DAY

The stork is a central image in many Lithuanian beliefs. The large bird is thought to bring good luck to homes. On Stork Day, March 25, farmers stir their planting seeds to increase the seeds' germinating power. It is said that snakes come out of their holes on this day. People avoid cutting wood or breaking off a branch, so as not to attract snakes to their homes.

other figurines. The tradition of Santa Claus or the Old Man of Christmas giving presents to children also started about this time.

Christmas Day is considered sacred and is celebrated more quietly. People sing hymns and carols and visit each other to exchange greetings.

FOLK MUSIC FESTIVALS

The best folk music performers are concentrated in Vilnius. Among the many folk music festivals held there, Skamba, *skamba kankliai* (skahm-ba, skahm-ba kan-kli-eye), held in the last week of May, is the most popular.

The largest folk singing festival is the Baltica Festival, held in a different Baltic city every year. The festival brings together singers and spectators from the three Baltic states and sometimes from Scandinavia as well. At the Baltica Festival in 1987, the flags of Lithuania, Latvia, and Estonia were displayed together for the first time since the Soviet occupation.

ISLAMIC FESTIVALS

The Tatars celebrate two important Islamic festivals.

Aidul-Fitr is celebrated right after Ramadan, which is one month of daily fasting between sunrise and sunset. The date varies, as the Islamic

The Feast of the Visitation in early July is marked by ten days of pilgrimages to Zemaiciu Kalvarija, one of the most revered religious and spiritual sites in Lithuania.

lunar calendar moves back 11 days each year in relation to the Gregorian calendar used in the West. Houses are thoroughly cleaned, and new clothes are made and worn to morning prayers in the mosque. In the evenings families come together to eat, exchange good wishes and presents, and to ask for forgiveness for any misunderstanding during the past 12 months.

Aidul-Adha is the feast of Abraham. It commemorates Abraham's being asked by God to sacrifice his son. Animal sacrifices are offered and the meat is distributed to friends, relatives, and the poor. A special prayer is said in the mosques early in the morning.

Lithuanians can now celebrate important days related to their history as a grand duchy and as an independent nation. Here people in traditional dress march in Vilnius to remember the devastating Soviet invasion of Lithuania in June 1940.

FOOD

LITHUANIAN CUISINE, based mainly on potatoes, is rich and somewhat fatty. It is straightforward fare not far removed from the foods of the countryside, but it is not as plain as the foods of Latvia and Estonia. The influence of the Tatars, Russians, Belorussians, and Poles is evident in the use of mild spices. Typical seasonings are caraway, garlic, onion, parsley, parsnip, dill, coriander, celery root, mustard, horseradish, fennel, and lovage (an herb of the carrot family).

Dishes vary in Lithuania according to the season. Animals are usually slaughtered in the fall and winter, so more meat is eaten at those times. During spring and summer, people consume more milk, vegetables, berries, mushrooms, and flour-based dishes. Fish from rivers, lakes, and the sea is abundant. The country's natural resources are well used, and there has always been an abundant supply of good food.

Left: **Shopping for the freshest strawberries in Vilnius.**

Opposite: **An elderly woman selling legumes at her stand in the Turganiete bazaar in Vilnius.**

Still warm loaves of dark rye bread for sale. The strong, sweet-sour taste of rye bread is ideally suited to the local beer, bland cheeses, and pungent cured meat and fish.

RYE BREAD

Lithuanians are very fond of dense bread made from dark rye flour, and they eat it at every meal. White wheat bread is baked only on special occasions.

If the bread is baked at home, the loaves are put on cabbage or calamus (sweet flag) leaves when baking, which imparts a special fragrance to the bread.

Bakers bake large oblong loaves, covered with maple, cabbage, or sweet flag leaves to add flavor. The sign of the cross as a blessing is made by the baker over the first loaf in a batch, and an impression of a cross is pressed into the last one.

Baking day is considered to be a special occasion, during which homes are quiet and no one argues for fear that the bread won't rise. If visitors arrive on baking day, they cannot leave until the baking is done so they can take a warm loaf home with them.

There are many superstitions associated with bread. A loaf of bread is inserted into the foundations of a new house to ensure that the family never runs out of bread. Farmers always plow a piece of bread into the first furrow in spring. The farmer's wife places a piece of bread under the first sheaf of rye during harvesttime. When moving into a new house, a loaf of bread is carried into the house along with pictures of saints. The bread, covered with a towel, is always placed in a special place in the house. Newlyweds are greeted with loaves of bread at the threshold of homes they may visit. A bride always takes a loaf of bread and some leaven (yeast or fermented dough) from her mother's mixture to her husband's home as a starter for her own bread. Important visitors are greeted with a loaf of bread on a towel. Slicing bread is always the proper task of the head of the family.

During the honey harvest season, cheese is served with honey. Serving cheese with honey is considered a very special treat, honoring guests and friends.

MILK AND CHEESE

The dairy industry is very important in the Baltic states. Both fresh and sour milk are used in Lithuania. Milk is drunk sweet or curdled. Butter and fresh cheese are part of the everyday diet. Lithuanians make lots of soft and hard cheeses and a kind of cottage cheese called sweet cheese. This is made by boiling milk mixed with sugar and eggs, then adding a little curd into the boiling milk, thereby curdling all the milk. The curds are strained and caraway seeds are sometimes added for flavor. The mixture is then pressed into cheese.

Cheese is served with coffee on special occasions and at festive events. A special, dense, yellow cheese is made for the midsummer festival. Cheese is always served with buttered bread. It is also given as a present when visiting friends and relatives.

THE MANY USES OF THE POTATO

Potatoes were introduced into Lithuania in the 18th century and very soon became the most popular item on the Lithuanian plate. Lithuanians especially love boiled white potatoes served with sour or fresh milk. Potatoes are used in soups, dumplings, porridge, pancakes, and puddings. Grated potatoes are used to make sausages. A typical Lithuanian dish is boiled potatoes served with pounded and fried hemp seeds.

Each housewife has her favorite potato recipe. Potato pie is served with sour milk, cottage cheese, sour cream, and fried cubed bacon. Since the beginning of the 20th century, *cepelinai*, or zeppelins—potato dumplings in the shape of the zeppelin airship and stuffed with meat and onions—have become a favorite Lithuanian dish.

OTHER DISHES

The Lithuanian diet has become fairly uniform throughout the country, although certain dishes predominate in different regions. Zemaitians are still fond of all kinds of porridge and *kastinis* (KAH-sti-nis), a kind of butter. Dzukians specialize in buckwheat and mushroom dishes. Suvalkians delight in *skilandis* (ski-LAHN-dis), smoked pig's stomach or bladder filled with minced meat and seasoned with pepper, garlic, and sweet cottage cheese. Aukstaitians love their special large pancakes for breakfast.

Meat comes mostly from cattle, sheep, goats, and pigs, and less from fowl. Pork is the most common meat in the Lithuanian diet. Virtually every part of the pig is eaten, including the foot and the ear. Lean pork and bacon is boiled or baked. Meat is salted or smoked for longer storage. Freshwater fish is an important food source for those residing near rivers and lakes, while those along the seacoast enjoy many saltwater fish. Smoked fish is often sold at wayside stalls as a tasty form of fast food, while smoked eel is a special treat among the people of the Baltic coast. Eels are found in Kursiu Marios and some rivers and lakes, and they grow to be 4 feet (1.2 m) long and up to 9 pounds (4.1 kg) in weight.

Beets, cabbages, and turnips have long been a part of Lithuanian cuisine. Beet greens and roots are eaten freshly boiled or pickled, or used in soups. Cold beet soup, with sour milk, cucumbers, dill, and hard-cooked eggs is a popular dish in the hot summer months. Lithuania also has its own version of the hot Russian borscht, where mushrooms are added to the beet soup, and it is sometimes accompanied by rissoles (fried fish or meat cakes). Fresh or pickled cabbage soup is a common dish. Some 20 species of mushroom are eaten in Lithuania. They are used to flavor soups, especially beet soup, during Lent. A cream soup with vegetables, such as potatoes, peas, carrots, or cabbage, cooked with flour-dough dumplings or pasta, is frequently eaten for dinner.

Farm-fresh fruit and vegetables are bought daily at the markets.

DRINKS

Milk is the most commonly consumed beverage. Coffee is by far the most popular hot drink, with tea a distant second. Both coffee and tea are served without milk.

The most popular alcoholic drink is beer. Lithuanians started brewing beer in the 16th century. Today each of Lithuania's cities has its own brewery. Some of the breweries are Vilniaus Tauras (in Vilnius), Ragutis and Kauno Alus (Kaunas), Svyturys (Klaipeda), Gubernija (Siauliai), and Kalnapilis (Panevezys). Lithuanian beer is of high quality and is brewed stronger and sweeter than those found in Western Europe. Homemade beer is still brewed in some districts.

The head of the household begins a special meal by pouring a mug of beer from a pitcher and saying to the guests, "To your health. Drink, brothers, and celebrate!" He then spills a few drops, drinks the cup dry, fills it again and hands it to a guest. The gathered people reply, "Be healthy" and "To your health." In this fashion, the cup makes it way down the table.

Sweet commercial soft drinks are widely available. Lithuania's most distinctive beverage is *gira* (GEE-rah), a slightly alcoholic soft drink made from either rye bread or caraway seeds. Birch sap flavored with black-currant leaves is also popular as a drink.

Midus (MI-doos), or mead, is an weak alcoholic drink made from honey. The ancient drink is produced commercially today, although the original recipe has been lost. Lithuania also produces several types of liqueurs as well as vodka and champagne.

Milk is an important part of the Lithuanian diet, as a drink, in cooking, and in other dairy products such as ice cream, a favorite with young and old.

KITCHENS

In old country houses, woodstoves are still used (with a gas or electric stove as a standby). Fuel is the dry branches and chopped wood of fallen trees gathered from the forest. The stoves also keep the houses warm.

Homes always contain a cellar, even in high-rise buildings in cities. In the countryside, cellars are dug outside and covered with an earth mound. Winter provisions are kept in the cellars: potatoes, beets, carrots, cabbages, onions, pumpkins, squashes, apples, sauerkraut, pickled cucumbers, and dried mushrooms. Most housewives preserve fruit and berries picked from the garden or forest. These, too, are stored in the cellar.

In Lithuanian kitchens, a clay pot is used as a double boiler for making soups and zeppelins, and a potato grater (electric or hand-turned) is indispensable because meals made with grated potatoes are an everyday affair.

AT THE TABLE

Lithuanian dining customs are rigidly structured and strictly observed. Each family member has an assigned place at the table. The head of the household sits at the end by the wall in the place of honor. Traditionally, men sit on one side of the table with the women opposite them. Important guests are seated in the place of honor or beside it.

Should a visitor arrive unexpectedly while the family is at the table, the visitor greets the family with "*Skanaus*" (SKA-na-oos), or "*Bon appétit.*" If the father returns the greeting with "You are welcomed," the guest is invited to join them at the table. Should the returned greeting simply be "Thank you," however, the guest is not welcomed at the table. This is rare, though, as guests, travelers, or even beggars who arrive at mealtime are always invited to the table.

Meals always begin with the slicing of bread by the head of the household. The first slice, the heel, is passed to the eldest son. The passing of bread continues down the table until each member of the family has taken a slice of bread from the father's hand. The remaining unsliced bread stays on the table. The cut end of the bread should face the most important corner of the house. Alternatively, it could also be placed facing the sun. Placing the loaf upside down on the table must never be done as it is believed that act foretells that death will come to the household. Neither should the cut end of the bread face the door, or madness will afflict the women and they will leave the home. Slices of bread are always broken with two hands because making the bread requires two hands. Lithuanians pride themselves on their hospitality and will relentlessly urge visitors to eat a little more. No one, even guests, rises from the table until everyone has finished eating.

VIRTO BULVIO KUKULIAI GRYBO PADATHE
(POTATO DUMPLINGS IN MUSHROOM SAUCE)

For the dumplings:
2 pounds (907 grams) potatoes, boiled
    or baked and peeled
1 cup flour
½ cup breadcrumbs
2 eggs, beaten with a pinch of salt
Several springs of parsley or dill, chopped
2 teaspoons salt

For the mushroom sauce:
1 teaspoon butter
1 cup fresh mushrooms (cut)
3 ounces bacon, finely diced
1 medium onion, finely diced
4 tablespoons sour cream

Mash the peeled potatoes in a bowl. Add the flour, breadcrumbs, eggs, and chopped herbs to the bowl. Mix the ingredients well. Knead the mixture until it becomes a soft dough. Make walnut-size dumplings with the dough. Minced meat can also be wrapped inside the dumplings. Bring several quarts of water to a boil in a large pot. Add two teaspoons of salt to the boiling water before dropping the dumplings one by one into it. Do not overfill the pot with dumplings and make sure that the water is always boiling. Stir occasionally. The dumplings are done when they rise to the surface, about 10 minutes after they are first put in the water. Lift out the cooked dumplings with a strainer. Place these in a serving dish and cover to keep warm.

To make the mushroom sauce, stir-fry the mushrooms in butter. Then add the bacon and onion. Once the onion is soft, add sour cream to the mixture. Reduce heat and cook five minutes more. Cover the dumplings with the mushroom sauce. Serve immediately.

SPANGUOLIU DREBUCIAI (CRANBERRY PUDDING)

2 cups cranberries
2 pieces stick cinnamon
4 whole cloves
1 cup sugar
1 cup potato starch (or 2 tablespoons cornstarch)
1 cup chilled cranberry juice

Place the cranberries in a 2-quart pot. Fill the pot with water until it covers the cranberries. Add the cinnamon and cloves. Heat over a medium flame until the berries begin to break up, about 15 minutes. Remove the pot from the heat and drain the juice and cranberries into a sieve over a waiting bowl. Mash the berries through the sieve, retaining only the pulp and juice. Discard the leftover skin, cloves, and cinnamon. Return the juice and pulp mixture to the pot. Add the sugar. Combine the starch with the chilled cranberry juice and add to the mixture. Over a low flame, bring the mixture to a gentle boil. Simmer, stirring constantly, until the mixture turns clear. Pour the hot pudding into individual bowls or glasses. Cool. When it turns to gel, it is ready to eat. May be served with whipped cream if desired.

Makes six to eight servings.

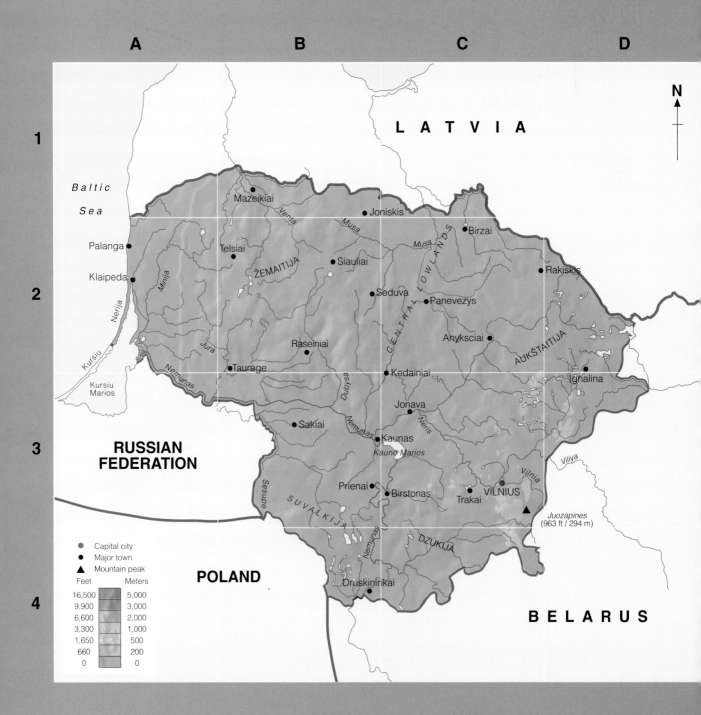

MAP OF LITHUANIA

Anyksciai, C2
Aukštaitija, region, C2

Baltic Sea, A1
Belarus, B4, C4,
   D2–D4, E2–E4
Birstonas, C3
Birzai, C2

Central Lowlands, C2

Druskininkai, B4
Dubysa River, B3
Dzúkija, region, C3

Ignalina, D3

Jonava, C3
Joniskis, B1
Juozapines, hill, C3
Jura River, A2

Kaunas, B3
Kauno Marios (Kaunas
   Lagoon), C3
Kedainiai, C2
Klaipeda, A2
Kursiu Marios, Kaunas
   Lagoon, A3
Kursiu Nerija National
   Park, A3

Latvia, A1, B1, C1–C2,
   D1–D2, E1–E2

Mazeikiai, B1
Minija River, A2
Musa River, B2

Nemunas River, A2
Neris River, C3

Palanga, A2
Panevezys, C2
Poland, A4
Prienai, B3

Rakiskis, C2
Raseiniai, B2
Russia, E1–E2
Russian Federation, A3

Sakiai, B3
Seduva, B2
Sesupe River, B3
Siauliai, B2
Suvalkija, region, B3

Taurage, B2
Telsiai, B2
Trakai, C3

Venta River, B1
Viliya River, D3
Vilnia River, C3
Vilnius, C3

Žemaitija, region, B2

ECONOMIC LITHUANIA

Manufacturing

- Electronics
- Food Processing
- Furniture Making
- Petroleum Refinery
- Shipbuilding
- Textiles

Natural Resources

- Amber
- L Limestone
- Sand

Services

- Airport
- Seaport
- Tourism

Agriculture

- Cattle Farming
- Fishing
- Potatoes
- Sugar Beets
- Vegetables

ABOUT
THE ECONOMY

OVERVIEW
Lithuania has made steady progress in developing a market economy since its independence in 1991. The success of its land and economic reforms, such as privatizing over 80 percent of state-owned property, is evident in its rapid economic growth. In the second quarter of 2006, its economic development grew to 8.4 percent. The majority of Lithuania's trade is with European Union countries. Lithuania has a well-developed transportation infrastructure and a skilled workforce. Its current unemployment rate at 5.7 percent is lower than in previous years. Lithuania is also agriculturally self-sufficient. Lithuania became a member of the World Trade Organization (WTO) in 2001 and the EU in May 2004.

GROSS DOMESTIC PRODUCT (GDP)
$54.9 billion (2006 estimate)

GDP GROWTH
7.5 percent (2006 estimate)

LAND USE
Arable land 44.81 per cent, permanent crops 0.9 per cent, others 54.29 per cent (2005 estimate)

CURRENCY
1 Lithuanian litas (LTL) = 100 centai
Notes: 500; 200; 100; 50; 20; 10 LTL
Coins: 50; 20; 10; 5; 2; 1 centai
1 USD = 2.53 LTL (August 2007)

NATURAL RESOURCES
Peat, arable land, gravel, construction sand, quartz sand, dolomite, clay, limestone, brick clay, amber.

AGRICULTURAL PRODUCTS
Grain, potatoes, sugar beets, flax, vegetables, cattle, milk, eggs, fish

INDUSTRIES
Metal-cutting machine tools, electric motors, television sets, refrigerators and freezers, petroleum refining, shipbuilding, furniture making, textiles, food processing, fertilizers, agricultural machinery, optical equipment, electronic components, computers, amber jewelry

MAJOR EXPORTS
Mineral products, machinery and equipment, light industrial exports such as textiles and food products, wood and wood products

MAJOR IMPORTS
Mineral products, machinery and equipment, chemicals, light industrial products like textiles

MAJOR TRADE PARTNERS
Russia, Germany, Poland, Latvia, Estonia

WORKFORCE
1.61 million (2006)

UNEMPLOYMENT RATE
5.7 percent (2006)

INFLATION RATE
3.8 percent (2006)

CULTURAL LITHUANIA

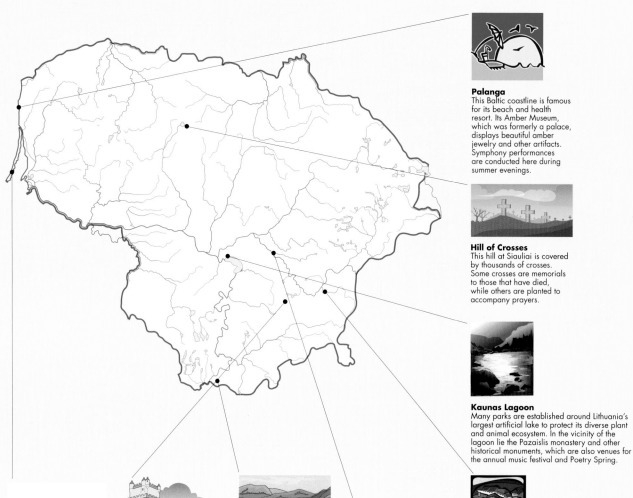

Palanga
This Baltic coastline is famous for its beach and health resort. Its Amber Museum, which was formerly a palace, displays beautiful amber jewelry and other artifacts. Symphony performances are conducted here during summer evenings.

Hill of Crosses
This hill at Siauliai is covered by thousands of crosses. Some crosses are memorials to those that have died, while others are planted to accompany prayers.

Kaunas Lagoon
Many parks are established around Lithuania's largest artificial lake to protect its diverse plant and animal ecosystem. In the vicinity of the lagoon lie the Pazaislis monastery and other historical monuments, which are also venues for the annual music festival and Poetry Spring.

Curonian Spit
Formed by sand drifts, this spit in the Neringa municipality is a narrow and isolated sandbar. Within the municipality lie four villages. Fishing and Jet Skiing are popular activities here.

Trakai Island Castle
Located on an island on Lake Galve, this Gothic castle was constructed in the 1400s. A moat separates the main tower from the courtyard where numerous concerts and plays are staged. The tower is also home to the Trakai History Museum.

Druskininkai
This picturesque spa town on the Nemunas River has seven mineral springs surrounded by natural forest reserves. The springs' high saline content is used in the treatment of nervous system disorders, among others. In 2003 Druskininkai was voted as one of the ten leading spa towns in Europe.

Kernave Archaeological and Historical Museum
Many artifacts ranging from Stone Age arrowheads to medieval jewelry are housed here. The museum is situated beside a neo-Gothic parish church. Every July, the Living Archaeology Days Festival is held in the village.

Old Town
This World Heritage Site in Vilnius has over 1,000 protected Baroque, Gothic, Renaissance, and Neoclassical monuments. The heart of the town, Pilies Street, has many street markets and cafés.

ABOUT THE CULTURE

OFFICIAL NAME
Lietuvos Respublika (Republic of Lithuania)

FLAG DESCRIPTION
Three equal horizontal bands of yellow (topmost), green and red.

TOTAL AREA
25,174 square miles (65,200 square km) of land

CAPITAL
Vilnius

POPULATION
3.6 million (2006 estimate)

ETHNIC GROUPS
Lithuanian 83.45 percent, Polish 6.74 percent, Russian 6.31 percent, Belorussians 1.23 percent, others (including Latvian, Jew, Tatar, Gypsy, German) 2.27 percent (2005 estimates)

RELIGIOUS GROUPS
Roman Catholic 79 percent, Russian Orthodox 4.1 percent, Protestant (including Lutheran and Evangelical Christian Baptist) 1.9 percent, Sunni Muslim 0.08 percent, other or unspecified 14.92 percent (2005 estimates)

BIRTHRATE
8.87 births per 1,000 Lithuanians (2007 estimate)

DEATH RATE
11.05 deaths per 1,000 Lithuanians (2007 estimate)

AGE STRUCTURE
0–14 years: 14.9 percent (male 273,573/ female 259,570)
15–64 years: 69.3 percent (male 1,213,011/ female 1,264,996)
65 years and over: 15.8 percent (male 194,500/ female 369,789) (2007 estimates)

LANGUAGES
Lithuanian (official), Russian, Polish, English, others (including Latvian, Belorussian, German, French)

LITERACY RATE
People ages 15 and above who can read and write: 99.6 percent (2007 estimate)

LEADERS IN POLITICS
Antanas Smetona: first president of independent Lithuania (1919–20; 1926–40)
Vytautas Landsbergis: leader of the Supreme Council after restoration of Lithuanian independence (1990–92)
Kazimira Prunskiene: first prime minister after restoration of Lithuanian independence (1990–91)
Algirdas Brazauskas: first post-Soviet president (1992–98)
Valdas Adamkus: president (1998–2003; 2004 to present)
Gediminas Kirkilas: prime minister since July 2006

TIME LINE

IN LITHUANIA	IN THE WORLD

2500 B.C.
Indo-European tribes settle along the Baltic shoreline of present-day Lithuania.

753 B.C.
Rome is founded.

116–17 B.C.
The Roman Empire reaches its greatest extent, under Emperor Trajan (98–17).

A.D. 100 – 900
The Lithuanians develop a prosperous trading empire with the Romans that covers northeastern Europe.

A.D. 600
Height of the Mayan civilization

1000
The start of feudalism in the Baltic region. The Lithuanians, the largest tribe, emerge dominant.

1000
The Chinese perfect gunpowder and begin to use it in warfare.

1236 – 1253
King Mindaugas unites the small feudal states of Lithuania into a duchy.

1392 – 1430
Under Grand Duke Vytautas's rule, Lithuania becomes one of the largest states in Europe.

1530
Beginning of transatlantic slave trade organized by the Portuguese in Africa.

1569
Lithuania and Poland form the Union of Lublin, sharing the same government.

1620
Pilgrims sail the *Mayflower* to America.

1776
U.S. Declaration of Independence

1795
Lithuania is absorbed by Russia, and military uprisings against Russian rule begins.

1789–99
The French Revolution

1891
Russia imposes a press ban on books and papers printed in Lithuanian.

1869
The Suez Canal is opened.

1915
German troops occupy Lithuania during World War I.

1914
World War I begins.

1918
Lithuania proclaims its independence on February 16. Antanas Smetona is elected its first president.

IN LITHUANIA	IN THE WORLD
1922	**1939**
A democratic constitution is adopted and the litas becomes the national currency.	World War II begins.
1941–44	
German army occupies Lithuania. The Nazis send hundreds of thousands of Lithuanian Jews to death camps.	
1944	**1945**
The Soviet Union absorbs Lithuania under its Communist regime.	The United States drops atomic bombs on Hiroshima and Nagasaki.
	1949
1988	The North Atlantic Treaty Organization (NATO) is formed.
The Lithuanian Movement for Reconstruction (Sajudis) is established.	
1990	
The Lithuanian Communist Party and the Sajudis declare the independence of the Republic of Lithuania.	
1991	**1991**
Soviet military crackdown on Lithuanian independence continues until August. In September, the Soviet government recognizes Lithuania's independence. In the same month, Lithuania joins the United Nations.	Breakup of the Soviet Union
1993	
Lithuania joins the Council of Europe and the litas is reintroduced as the national currency. Soviet troops withdraw completely from Lithuania.	**1997**
	Hong Kong is returned to China.
1998	
Valdas Adamkus is elected president; formal negotiations to join NATO and the EU begin.	**2001**
	Terrorists crash planes in New York, Washington, D.C., and Pennsylvania.
2004	**2003**
Lithuania joins NATO in March and in May, the EU. One reactor at the Ignalina nuclear power station shuts down. The second one is due to close by 2009.	War in Iraq begins.

GLOSSARY

birbynes (beer-BEE-nus)
A reed whistle

delmonas (dayl-MOH-nus)
A traditional decorative handbag

gira (GEE-rah)
A slightly alcoholic soft drink made from either rye bread or caraway seeds

glasnost
Openness; a Soviet reform policy of the 1980s

jonkelis (YONG-kay-lis)
A Lithuanian dance

kaledaiciai (kah-le-DY-chi-eye)
Christmas Eve wafers

kankles (KAHN-klis)
A traditional stringed musical instrument

kastinis (KAH-sti-nis)
A kind of butter popular in Zemaitija

klumpes (KLOOM-pus)
Traditional wooden shoes

Kucios (KOO-chi-ohs)
Christmas Eve

lamždelis (lum-zhe-DAY-lis)
A wooden recorder

midus (MI-doos)
Mead, an ancient alcoholic drink made of honey

patarle (PAH-tehr-lay)
A proverb; a brief wise observation

perestroika
Restructuring; a Soviet reform policy of the 1980s

polytheism
The worshipping of many gods

raudos (RAO-dohs)
Laments or farewell songs

Sajudis (SAH-yoo-dis)
A political organization that advocated Lithuanian independence

salde (SAHL-day)
A soft drink cordial made from rye

Seimas (SAY-i-mahs)
The Lithuanian parliament

skilandis (ski-LAHN-dis)
A dish of smoked pig's stomach or bladder stuffed with seasoned meat

šustas (SHOOS-tahs)
A Lithuanian dance

Užgavenes (OO-zhe-GAH-veh-nes)
Shrovetide festival

Vytis (VEE-tis)
The charging white knight on a white horse that is the state emblem of Lithuania

žekelis (ZHAY-kay-lis)
A Lithuanian dance

zeppelin
A potato dumpling filled with meat and onions

FURTHER INFORMATION

BOOKS

Alfonsas Eidintas. *Jews, Lithuanians and the Holocaust.* Vilnius, Lithuania: Versus Aureus, 2003.

Docalavich, Heather. *Lithuania.* Philadelphia, PA: Mason Crest Publishers, 2006.

Government of Lithuania. *Lithuania: An Outline.* Vilnius, Lithuania: Akreta UAB, 2002.

Lane, Thomas. *Lithuania: Stepping Westward.* London and New York: Routledge, 2002.

Milosz, Czeslaw. *New and Collected Poems, 1931–2001.* London: Allen Lane/Penguin Press, 2001.

Suziedelis, Saulius. *Historical Dictionary of Lithuania.* Lanham, MD.: Scarecrow Press, 1997 (also available as an e-book).

Williams, Nicola, Becca Blond, Regis St. Louis. *Estonia, Latvia & Lithuania.* London: Lonely Planet Publications, 2006.

WEB SITES

Baltic Times, The. News from Latvia, Estonia and Lithuania. www.baltictimes.com

Central Intelligence Agency World Factbook (select Lithuania from country list). www.cia.gov/cia/publications/factbook

Embassy of the Republic of Lithuania to the USA. www.ltembassyus.org/

Lithuania—In Your Pocket City Guide. www.inyourpocket.com/lithuania/en/

Lithuanian Classic Literature Anthology. http://anthology.lms.lt/

Lithuanian Poetry in English Translation. www.efn.org/~valdas/poezija.html

Lituanus, Lithuanian Quarterly Journal of Arts and Sciences. www.lituanus.org/

Lonely Planet World Guide: Lithuania. www.lonelyplanet.com/worldguide/destinations/europe/lithuania

Medieval Lithuania, edited by Tomas Baranauskas. http://viduramziu.lietuvos.net/en/

U.S. Department of State: Lithuania. www.state.gov/r/pa/ei/bgn/5379.htm

FILMS

Algimantas Puipa. *Elze's Life.* Lietuvos Kino Studija, 1999.

Jonas Mekas. *Reminiscences of a Journey to Lithuania.* 1972.

Jonas Viatkus. *Utterly Alone.* Vilnius: V & K Holding, 2004.

MUSIC

Songs and Dances from Lithuania. Dainava, 2001.

Songs by Lithuanian Composers. Lyra Classics, 2003.

Vel: Lithuanian Chamber Music. Guild, 2005.

BIBLIOGRAPHY

Avizienis, Raza and William Hough. *Guide to Lithuania*. Guilford, CT: The Globe Pequot Press, 1995.

Chicoine, Stephen and Brent K. Ashabranner. *Lithuania: The Nation that Would Be Free*. New York: Cobblehill, 1995.

Harbor, Bernard. *The Breakup of the Soviet Union*. East Sussex: Wayland, U.K., 1992.

Insight Guides: Baltic States. Hong Kong: APA Publications, 1994.

Government of the Republic of Lithuania. www.lrv.lt/main_en.php

Library of Congress, Federal Research Division, Country Studies—Lithuania. http://lcweb2.loc.gov/frd/cs/lttoc.html

McLachlan, Gordon. *Lithuania: The Bradt Travel Guide*. Old Saybrook, CT: Bradt, The Globe Pequot Press, 2005.

Statistics Lithuania. www.stat.gov.lt/en/

INDEX